Learning Linocut

A Comprehensive Guide to the Art of Relief Printing through Linocut

by Susan Yeates

www.learninglinocut.co.uk

Visit us online at www.authorsonline.co.uk

A Bright Pen Book

Copyright © Susan Yeates 2011

Cover design by Susan Yeates ©
Cover images: 'The Great Spotted Woodpecker' by Max Angus, 'Red Tractor' by Anthony Dyson, 'Broadstairs Catch' by Andy Johnson, 'Deal' by Colin Moore.

All rights reserved. No part of this publication may be reproduced, stored in a retrieval system, or transmitted in any form or by any means, electronic, mechanical, photocopy, recording or otherwise, without prior written permission of the copyright owner. Nor can it be circulated in any form of binding or cover other than that in which it is published and without similar condition including this condition being imposed on a subsequent purchaser.

British Library Cataloguing in Publication Data.
A catalogue record for this book is available from the British Library.

ISBN: 978-0-7552-1523-2

Authors OnLine Ltd
19 The Cinques
Gamlingay, Sandy
Bedfordshire SG19 3NU
England

This book is also available in e-book format, details of which are available at www.authorsonline.co.uk

Contents

Introduction — 5

Chapter 1: Getting Started — 9
- Inspiration, Ideas and Imagination — 9
- Studio Space — 19
- Materials for Linocut Printing — 25
- Relief Press or Hand-Burnishing? — 34

Chapter 2: Linocut Basics — 37
- Block Preparation and Basic Cutting — 38
- Mark-Making — 43
- Image Interpretation — 46
- One-Colour Printing — 51
- Registration — 55

Chapter 3: Advanced Techniques — 59
- Reduction Technique - 'The Suicide Print' — 60
- Multiple Plate Printing - Key-Block — 66
- Inking Techniques and Tips — 73
- Experimental Linocut — 78

Chapter 4: The Finished Linocut — 87
- Editioning — 88
- Presenting and Storing Work — 88
- Selling Your Work — 94

Chapter 5: Linocut Projects and Resources — 97
- Project 1: 'In the Style of...' — 98
- Project 2: Old Photograph — 99
- Project 3: Book Illustration — 100
- Project 4: A Patchwork Print — 101
- Useful Resources — 102

www.magenta-sky.com

This book is dedicated to all the people who have inspired me to be the person that I am today and to those who have helped me to realise that you can achieve anything that you set your mind to.

Acknowledgements

Thank you to all the printmakers who have kindly contributed images to this book. I would also like to mention all the students who have attended my workshops and classes and had so much enthusiasm and all the art teachers and tutors who have taught me in the past. I am very grateful to Ochre Print Studio and Otters Pool Studio for the use of your facilities. And finally a big thank you to all my friends and family for your support and encouragement.

Introduction

Welcome to Learning Linocut!

"This book, as suggested by its title, is intended to provide a comprehensive guide to linocut. Whether you are a complete beginner to art, just new to printmaking or you are an accomplished printmaker looking for some new ideas and tips, there will be something in here for you to take away.

Linocut is a fascinating and versatile technique that I began personally several years ago due to having no access to a professional printmaking studio. It was the ideal technique to use in a small space at home and once I started, I was hooked!

Learning Linocut entirely focuses on the art of relief printing using lino in a way that no other book on the subject does. Rather than simply providing a step-by-step guide on how to cut and print a lino print, this book explores the whole creative process from generating your ideas through to finally displaying and selling your work. Alongside this are a selection of my own prints, works by students that have attended workshops and linocuts by other printmakers who have kindly allowed their work to be reproduced here as fine examples of the possibilities of the technique.

In **Chapter 1** we explore in detail how to generate ideas for your prints as well as discussing the materials used and setting up your own studio space. In **Chapter 2** we take you through the basics of linocut from cutting techniques and mark-making, to image interpretation and simple one-colour printing. **Chapter 3** advances on this by exploring ways of creating multiple-colour prints through the reduction technique, the key-block system and also experimental relief print. **Chapter 4** investigates ways of storing, finishing, editioning and selling your prints. Finally **Chapter 5** will provide some interesting linocut projects for you to try out your new skills.

The concept of *Learning Linocut* actually developed from a series of factsheets and course materials that I have used over the years when teaching printmaking in various classes and workshops. Therefore, included in the book are several popular exercises that build up your linocutting skills and the answers to many of the regular questions I get asked. There are also plenty of little gems of information discovered through my own experience and through talking to other printmakers that I will share within these pages.

I hope you enjoy reading this book and wish you happy printmaking!"

Susan Yeates, Printmaker

> **Susan's Tip...**
>
> "Look out for my tips and suggestions throughout the book. These will be placed in boxes just like this and provide a selection of helpful pointers on the topic being discussed."

What is Printmaking?

Printmaking is essentially the process of creating an original 'print', by transferring an impression from one surface to another. In other words it is not a direct process such as drawing or painting but any method that allows an artist to create an image in one place that is then transferred to another. Prints are usually created onto paper but experimenting with other materials is very common.

The dictionary definition of a print is: **Print (noun) -** A mark made by pressing something onto a surface.

However, prints in the context of printmaking are designed and created by printmakers and classed as **original prints**. These prints are not reproductions of original works, but original works in their own right. They can be one-offs such as monoprints or have a much larger number of identical or near identical images (called an edition) such as linoprints.

The process of creating a print is called printmaking and the technique of linocut is just one of the many techniques that can be used.

History of Printmaking

Printmaking has a fascinating history since it has both ancient precedents and yet, as an art form in its own right, is still relatively new. We know that cavemen began engraving rocks, walls and stone tablets early in history, but the first instance of transferring engraved images originates in the Far East, where it appears rubbing was used by the Chinese between the 1st and 2nd century AD. In Japan, the use of woodcut to print was used in the 8th century to produce religious rubbings.

▶ Textile and Paper

The majority of early printmaking was concerned with the transfer and duplication of text and pictures onto textiles, but gradually printing onto paper became the dominant medium. This was widespread throughout both Europe and the Far East by the 15th century. In Europe, this century saw the use of royal seals and stamps on documents. However, printmaking did not always serve such a 'serious' purpose as the commercial production of playing cards using the technique was also observed during this period.

'ROOFTOPS' (LINOCUT), SUSAN YEATES, 2008 - 7CM x 16CM

'MERSEA I' (4-COLOUR LINOCUT), COLIN MOORE, 2008 - 46CM x 46CM

As metalwork production increased in this period, so did the use of printing from engravings on a metal surface, which produced prints with much finer detailing. By the late 15th century, engraving and etching had established themselves as the two most popular printmaking techniques, with the latter's simplicity in application (requiring no formal metalwork training) making it accessible to all types of artist. Albrecht Dürer (1471-1528) was a prominent and prolific printmaker of the period using all of the above techniques throughout his career.

During the 17th and 18th century, European printmaking developed in technique, expanded the use of processes and flourished throughout the continent. In England, William Hogarth (1697-1764) set the standard for British printmaking, especially through his moral series, such as 'The Harlot's Progress' and 'The Rake's Progress'. Here, printmaking can be seen to serve a clear purpose. With its moralising subject matter, printmaking allowed the series to reach a far wider audience than the original oil paintings could on their own and arguably made them more accessible to the 'ordinary person in the street' to whom they were aimed.

▶ A 'Serious' Art Form

By the 18th century, printmaking had begun to establish itself as a 'serious' art form. However, a degree of prejudice still existed then as today where many art history courses still talk of the three traditional 'high art' forms of painting, sculpture and architecture. Printmaking was seen by some as 'craft' or 'low art' in the 18th century. Though it was gradually taken seriously by an increasing number of patrons and buyers who put a high value on original prints. During the 19th century, printmaking established itself further with artists signing their work and producing limited, numbered editions of their prints.

▶ Modern Printmaking

The radical changes in art during the 20th century were shared in printmaking and the use of its techniques was found in the work of many artists. Pablo Picasso (1881-1973) embraced the technique throughout his career whilst printmaking dramatically entered popular culture through the work of pop artists like Andy Warhol (1928-1987). With Pop Art, printmaking had its unique qualities once again used to the full in expressing both subject and meaning. If Pop Art reflected the look and feel of consumer, mass-produced images, then printmaking was the natural choice to reflect the power of strong imagery and duplication.

▶ Printmaking Today

Throughout the 20th century and into the 21st century, techniques have developed and been refined. As the 'evergreen' art form it is no surprise that digital printmaking has been harmoniously incorporated into the range of techniques and processes available to the printmaker.

Learning Linocut | p7

Relief Printing

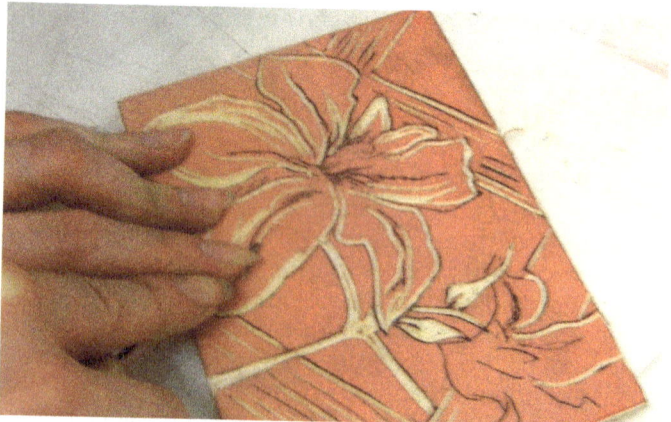

CARVING INTO A WOODCUT BLOCK

As already mentioned, there are many forms of printmaking but in this book we are specifically focusing on linocut, which is a form of relief printing.

Relief printing is a collection of negative techniques where the plate or block is cut into using knives, gouges or chisels to create an image. The area that is left uncut is what prints and the cut out area does not print. The final print will also be a 'mirror image' of the original plate. Relief blocks can be printed by hand or using a press. Several blocks can be prepared to produce multiple coloured prints. Relief processes include linocut, woodcut and wood engraving but also loosely techniques such as collograph.

▶ What is Linocut?

Linocut is a form of relief printing that uses linoleum as the printing block (a composite flooring material made from cork and linseed oil with a hessian backing). The smooth surface of the lino allows for ease of cutting in all directions and is specially produced for artists to use. The ink sits on the relief of the lino before printing and is transferred onto paper through rubbing on the back by hand or by using a printing press. Lino is usually thin enough (3-5mm) to be placed through an etching press as well as printing in a relief press.

Linocut is a technique with endless possibilities for experimentation and creativity. The concept of printing a lino block is quite simple and the results quite immediate, but with a little practice and exploration, some incredibly complex and rich results can be produced.

Linocut seems to satisfy methodical and technical printmakers whist leaving plenty of room for creativity, experimentation and a quick result. It is an enjoyable mix of skilled control of a technique and a certain element of what we term the 'happy accident'.

There are certain marks and effects produced through linocut (and woodcut) that just cannot be created using other methods such as painting or drawing. Linocuts are often recognised by their bold 'cutting' marks and striking use of flat colours layered over each other. Whilst reading this book, try to seek out linocut works that inspire you and demonstrate how creatively linocut is used by other printmakers.

Through the next few chapters we will take you on an exciting tour of the process of working with linocut. This tour will be detailed, practical and more importantly accompanied by colour pictures of finished prints and works in progress, step-by-step guides and lists of materials needed.

Chapter 1: Getting Started

Inspiration, Ideas and Imagination

Before we explain the technique of linocut from a technical perspective, it is important to start thinking about the subject matter of your prints and the ways in which you will gather ideas to work from.

Collating ideas and imagery will often be an ongoing process or continued exploration of a particular theme or style, therefore for the purposes of this book it is the place that we will start.

Using your creativity and imagination to produce stimulating prints that will interest a viewer is all part of the process of being a printmaker. Whether you are a beginner to printmaking and need help to find images to work from or are an experienced artist looking to explore new methods, there should be something in this chapter to help unlock your printmaking imagination!

We will look at general themes you could try, research trips, life drawing, drawing for print and the important ways that you actually experiment with this information such as by using sketchbooks and idea sheets.

Then, at the start of **Chapter 2** we will look at techniques for directly interpreting your research and inspiration into actual linocuts.

'AMOS' (LINOCUT), RICHENDA COURT, 2010 - 64CM x 48CM

▶ General Themes

There are so many themes or subject matters that can be explored through linocut – the list is endless and there are no limits. Whichever topic you select, make it one that you enjoy and feel inspired to create from. Maybe by looking at your favourite artist - the subject matter they use may inspire you too. Try some of the following topic suggestions…

- **Traditional Themes and Ideas**
Self-portraiture
Portraiture
Still Life
Landscapes
The city
Life and death
The body
The self

- **Personal Themes**
Your childhood
Your mother, father or family
Experiences from your past
Your children, childbirth
Your home
Your favourite sport, interest or hobby

- **Pattern, Shape and texture**
Colour
Materials and textured fabric
Pattern and shape
Light and dark
Black and white
Geometric

- **Nature**
Trees
Flowers
Allotments
Birds and animals
Water
Fish
Fruit and vegetables

- **Costume and Fashion**
Jewellery
Costume (contemporary or historical)
Fashion today
Textiles, fabric, dressmaking
Your favourite fashion designer

- **Art History / Architecture**
Ethnic design origins
Periods in Art history
Your favourite building
Your town / city

- **History and Politics**
Current political debate
Periods in history that inspire or interest you
War
A historical figure

- **Travel and Other Cultures**
A recent holiday
Your religion or culture
The sea
Images of other cultures and countries
A local place of interest or tourist spot

- **Literature and Drama**
Your favourite book, author or play
Themes from literature
Words
A famous quote
A news item

> ▶ **Susan's Tip…**
>
> "The list of topics is endless and this is by no means a definitive list! These are simply a starting point to work from, for example, you may have taken a photograph of a landscape and want to use it as a source for a print or collected some leaves and flowers from your garden that have interesting shapes and patterns that you can draw from."

▶ Words as a Starting Point

Sometimes simply a word will inspire an idea that you wish to explore. Choose (or randomly pick) one word listed here as a starting point...

movement

OLD

time

night

texture

shadows

BELONGING

faith

essence

LIFE

death

rhythm

home

lost

darkness

love

COMMUNITY

DREAMS

waiting

perspective

degradation

money

birth

Communication

function

scale

inspiration

childish

creativity

truth

dignity

What other words can you think of to inspire you?

SUCCESS

unity

INDUSTRIAL

freedom

newness

borders

GROWTH

SPACE

light

INSPIRING WORDS

DANGER

dance

generations

Learning Linocut | p11

▶ Research Trips

Research trips are a great way of either finding a topic for working on or developing a topic already started. There are many different places that you can visit to seek design ideas or inspiration. Try:

- Art exhibitions
- Museums
- Craft galleries
- University or college exhibitions or shows
- Heritage sites (castles, stately homes or cathedrals)
- Public gardens
- Tourist attractions
- Foreign countries and cultures

Wherever you choose to go and whatever inspires you, from an artist's work to a piece of furniture or architecture, it is essential you make the most of your visit. Allow yourself a reasonable amount of time to fully appreciate the exhibition or place of interest.

Take a sketchbook with you and jot down notes as you walk around. Spend some time immersing yourself in the atmosphere of the venue and write down what it is that inspires you or what you like and do not like about what you are looking at. Words in a sketchbook are just as useful as actual drawings.

Once you have taken in the general atmosphere, go back to study a particular work, item or place in more detail. Make several short sketches and then a longer more time-consuming study. Collect any literature from or about the venue to remind you of what you saw. Take some photographs too, if appropriate.

The purpose of regular research trips is to widen your knowledge of art, design and culture in general and more specifically provide a cultural framework for the prints you are working on. Regular research trips will help to balance out the technical and practical information on linocut this book will provide, with cultural and image-based design information.

▶ Life Drawing

If you carry out any work where you are drawing the human form it is highly recommended you try life drawing. Life drawing is a fantastic method for studying the human figure. Whether clothed or unclothed, time is spent drawing a model in a fixed position. This can vary from very quick one minute sketches to gain an impression of movement and the general shape, to much longer poses capturing much more detail, including light and shadow, hands, clothing and faces.

Life drawing will also gradually improve your observation and drawing skills through detailed study of the figure and regular practice of your drawing ability. If you are not very confident with your drawing skills, look for a beginners class near to you that can teach you basic drawing techniques and help get you started.

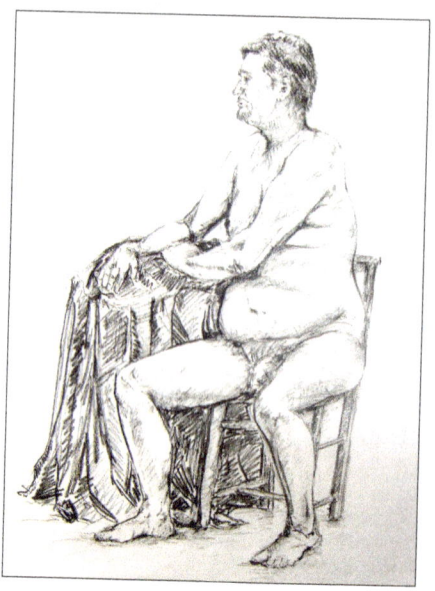

PENCIL DRAWING FROM A LIFE DRAWING CLASS

The drawings you create can again be used as part of an idea sheet or sketchbook or as the pure subject matter. It may be that you are creating a work with several people in it and you need to get the poses or facial expressions correct.

▶ Drawing for Printmaking

Drawing plays a vital part in any art form and this includes printmaking. Every person who reads this book will have a different drawing capability and will use drawing as part of their work to varying degrees. To some extent drawing is a very personal experience and some people will wish to draw a lot to fuel their ideas and prints, others will not.

As this is a 'Learning Linocut' book and not a 'Learning Drawing' book, the primary focus is to concentrate on linocut. However, this short section will quickly look at a few drawing exercises you can utilise when studying an object to help generate ideas and produce a series of interesting marks and shapes.

Once you have completed the exercises, or some of them, remember the way that the drawings were produced and try to use some of the techniques regularly to create interesting, free and fun sketches as part of your studies for a print.

▶ Tools and Materials

- 1 sheet of A1 cartridge paper
- Pencil (soft drawing pencil such as 2b, 3b or 4b)
- A small household object to draw
- Stopwatch or your own watch
- Craft knife or Stanley knife
- 1 smaller A3 sheet of cartridge paper
- Marker pen or drawing pen
- Charcoal

▶ Step-By-Step Guide

These exercises should take about half an hour to an hour to complete, so set aside some time and a space on a desk to work. You will benefit more by completing the exercises in one sitting.

1. Place your cartridge paper on your desk ready to use and make sure that your pencil is sharp.

2. Choose a small household item or object to draw from such as a bottle, ornament, cup, piece of fruit etc. Place it at the top of the paper ready to draw.

3. Working on just the one sheet of cartridge paper (do not turn it over or start a new one), work through the list of exercises below. If it means that at times you have to overlap the drawings, then do so. This is an exercise in creating interesting marks and ideas for prints and not a finished piece of work so try to switch off your mind and allow yourself to focus on the observation of your chosen object. Use the time guide to the right to limit the time you spend on each sketch, or ask someone to read out the exercises to you and time you.

▶ Table of Drawing Exercises

	Exercise	Time
1	Make a very quick pencil sketch of your object anywhere on the paper.	30 seconds
2	Turn the object to a different angle and make another quick sketch.	30 seconds
3	Turn the object a 3rd time and sketch again.	30 seconds
4	Now spend a little longer making a small sketch of the object - try to add a bit more detail to your sketch.	1 minute
5	Finally, make a longer sketch of your object picking out more detail, trying to capture any texture and interesting shapes.	2 minutes
6	Now take your pencil and move it from your drawing hand and place it in your non-drawing hand (i.e. left hand if you are right-handed). Draw the object at another angle for 1 minute using your wrong hand. Concentrate on the object and the shape of it to try and control the hand you are not used to using.	1 minute

	Exercise	Time
7	Now place the pencil back in your drawing hand and put the object right at the top of your sheet of paper or at a distance. Now draw the object without looking at the drawing you make. Usually when making a drawing you should look at the subject about 70% of the time, here you will be looking at it 100% of the time - observe the shape and your impression of the object in detail and try to translate detail to paper without looking at your drawing at all.	1 minute
8	As the complete opposite to this, remove the object out of your sight and try drawing the object from memory. i.e. with 100% of your time focused on looking at the paper and none at the object.	1 minute
9	Now hold the pencil at the very top away from the lead using just your index finger, middle finger and thumb, so that you have very limited control. Put the pencil at right angles to the paper and draw the object keeping the pencil straight.	1 minute
10	We will now do a 'spaghetti drawing'. This means that you will make a drawing using just one continuous line. Once your pencil touches the paper and you start the drawing, do not lift it up at all from the paper - you will use just one line to complete the whole drawing. If this means that you have to go back and trace over a line then do so.	1 minute
11	Switch to using a pen or marker pen instead of pencil and draw your object again at another angle and see what difference the different medium makes.	1 minute
12	Switch again to charcoal and draw it again.	1 minute
13	This time move the object again and using a pencil try drawing just the tone and shadows of the object - i.e. don't draw any lines or outlines but just the shade and light.	2 minutes

	Exercise	Time
14	Move the object to a different angle and draw it with as light a line as you can - the pencil should almost float across the paper - in some parts you may not even be able to see it because the line is so light.	1 minute
15	Now draw the object with an ANGRY line - imagine that you hate the object and really try and scribble your drawing down with force. Think strong, forceful, bold lines.	1 minute
16	Now draw the outline (or silhouette) of the object in a thin pencil line.	1 minute
17	Now repeat this drawing again 3-4 times without looking at the object again but just repeating your line drawing of the silhouette. Try to make each drawing touch the next so you have either a line of identical drawings or a square of 4 drawings.	2 minutes
18	Now draw the object as small as you can on the paper. Try to record as much detail as you can but imagine that someone will need to use a magnifying glass to see your small drawing properly.	1 minute
19	Now draw the object as large as you can on the paper - this drawing will probably overlap many of your drawings already - try to make it fill as much of the paper as you can and touch the edges of the paper if possible.	3 minutes

By the end of the series of exercises you should have a sheet of paper, packed with sketches of your chosen object. Many of the lines will overlap and you will have impressions of your object from many different angles. Due to the nature of the drawing exercises you will also be able to pick out a collection of interesting and contrasting lines from the sheet of paper. The lines have been generated from holding the pencil in a different way and would not have been created had you simply drawn the object over and over again in the same way.

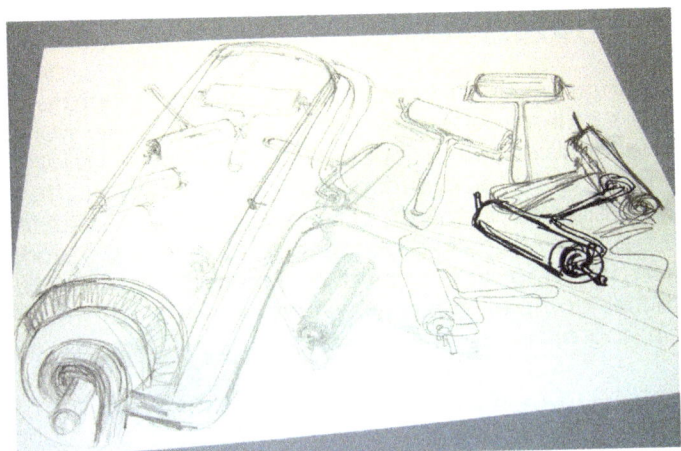

EXAMPLE OF A DRAWING SHEET USING A ROLLER AS THE OBJECT

The lines as they overlap will have created interesting shapes, not just of the object itself but of the spaces between where you have drawn as well (the negative space). This negative space can be a very interesting place from which to start a print and will also help you to begin thinking in the 'negative / positive' mindset of a printmaker that we will explain later on in the book for how to look at an image. Use this way of studying an object in detail and apply this to the way that you generally make sketches and drawings of a place, artwork or larger subject matter.

This drawing exercise is by no means the only way to generate imagery for linocutting but it helps to just give you a few ideas for how to look at an object you are studying.

▶ **Susan's Tip...**

"Sometimes just spending 10 minutes doing a few of these exercises before you start on your printmaking can warm you up ready to work and think creatively."

▶ Using a Paper 'Window' Frame

To help find interesting shapes and select an area of a drawing, sketch or painting to use, it can be very helpful to create a 'window' made from paper.

1. Take an A3 or A4 sheet of cartridge paper and fold it in half and then fold it in half again. In the folded corner, draw 2 straight pencil lines at right angles to create a square or rectangle. Using a craft knife cut along the 2 pencil lines to remove this piece paper from the centre of the sheet.

2. When you open up the sheet you will have a rectangular 'window' in the centre that will act as a frame to place over your images.

A PAPER 'WINDOW' PLACED OVER A DRAWING IN A SKETCHBOOK

3. Place the frame over the drawing sheet you have just created in the previous exercise or over a sketchbook. By moving the frame around, you will begin to find areas on the paper that will suit a print.

4. This framing exercise is incredibly useful and can also be used with any idea sheets or preparatory work to help you get the framing correct. It will also assist you in looking at photographs or cuttings from magazines in an alternative way. Create different sized frames for the different sized prints you wish to produce.

Learning Linocut | p15

▶ Newspapers and Magazines

Newspapers and magazines contain a wealth of images, photographs and do not forget stories and news items that you can use for your prints. Fashion and design magazines contain beautiful colour images that can be cut out and stuck into sketchbooks. It may be that a simple image, pattern, shape or pose of a model sparks an idea for a print.

Look out also for interesting news items that could act as a starting point for your work. You may be following a topical debate that you feel strongly about such as climate change, war, cultural or political issues and newspapers can provide a great source of information from which to base your work.

▶ Photography

Photography is a fantastic way to quickly generate a series of inspirational 'sketches' from which to work. Due to the nature of linocut (in that it can take a long time to carve out your image into the lino) it is often impossible to do this on location, making it helpful to use photography to make preparatory studies to work from. Photographs can also be used to generate more complex designs by combining two or more photographs into one final image.

Photographs can be traced directly, drawn from, edited in a design software package on your computer or incorporated into general sketchbook work or idea sheets.

'TIGER' (REDUCTION LINOCUT), ARLENE MUDIE, 2011
THIS LINOPRINT WAS PRODUCED DURING A 2-DAY LINOCUT WORKSHOP. THE INITIAL IMAGE USED FOR THE IDEA WAS A ROYALTY-FREE PHOTOGRAPH SOURCED ON THE INTERNET, PRINTED IN COLOUR AT THE CORRECT SIZE AND THEN THE TWO COLOURS OF THE REDUCTION WORKED OUT TO MATCH THE STRIKING COLOURS OF THE TIGER.

▶ Libraries and the Internet

These may seem obvious places for researching a topic but they are well worth mentioning. Your local library or larger libraries with a better stock of art books, are an essential visit at some point to help with development of a theme. You may need to find out more about a particular artist or subject matter to help you fully understand and reach certain conclusions.

The Internet provides a wealth of quickly accessible visual and text-based information at the click of a mouse, which can be printed or bookmarked for further study.

▶ Sketchbooks

Using a sketchbook or scrapbook is an essential way of grouping together your various thoughts, sketches and small pieces of visual information you want to keep to help feed your ideas and inspiration.

There are so many different sizes and shapes of sketchbooks available and each artist has their own preference. **A small A6 size sketchbook is good to carry around with you and keep a larger sketchbook for developing ideas further at home.** If you intend to use ink or paint you may need to find a sketchbook that has good quality paper inside. There are also many with handmade or textured paper.

Sketchbooks should always be very spontaneous and a way of keeping together any ideas you suddenly want to remember. Take note of the word 'sketch' – it is a book of sketches, whether these are in the form of drawings, photocopies, magazine cuttings or your written ideas. A sketchbook keeps all your ideas over a period of time together in one place and should be a varied and interesting collection for you to then start to progress an idea or two towards a final print.

When starting a sketchbook, just begin to gather cuttings and images that you like and stick them in. Make a quick note next to each image stating what you like about it and why. Try placing different images next to each other or draw over the top of a cutting or photo you have stuck in. Think about creating collages and try layering different things on top of each other to see the result.

The sketchbook is a very useful tool to come back to time and time again when you need inspiration or want to try something out first before printing it. They are also a great place to stick 'proofs' and prints 'gone wrong'. The sorts of things you can add to a sketchbook include:

- Pencil and pen drawings
- Newspaper and magazine cuttings
- Photographs or postcards
- Small watercolours or acrylic/gouache paintings
- Photocopies
- Your notes or something you want to look up later
- Proofs of your prints or prints 'gone wrong'
- Rubbings

A SELECTION OF SKETCHBOOKS

▶ Susan's Tip...
"I recommend that you start a sketchbook today!"

▶ Idea Sheets

An idea sheet (or mood board) is often used in many creative processes including textiles and interior design to develop an idea, theme or mood on a large single sheet of paper or card.

Whereas the sketchbook has the ability to be portable and informal, the idea sheet has the benefit of displaying a selection of ideas and developed themes in one place – a quick visual shot of your idea or 'mood'. They are often a more developed stage of the creative process. The sheet of paper should be covered with drawings and source materials that will help to inspire your print – maybe even the final design for your print is on here. It can also be propped up and viewed from afar to view its impact.

To create an idea sheet, firstly choose a topic or subject that you are investigating. Start to collect a large number of cuttings, sketches, paintings, photographs, postcards that relate to your topic or reflect the mood that you are trying to create. Sometimes this can even be a small piece of fabric, a colour swatch from a DIY store or samples of the inks that you may want to use in your linocut print. Then take a large sheet of cartridge paper (A2 or A1 sheets work well) and lay it in the middle of the desk on which you are working.

Begin to lay down the cuttings and drawings on the sheet without sticking them down. Place images next to each other in a way that complements and begins to create a complete 'mood'. Make sure that the individual items either overlap or are placed right up next to each other to completely fill the piece of paper – work right to the edges. When you are happy with the rough placement, begin to stick the items down using glue or tape. Sometimes patterns drawn on tracing paper or acetate placed over other drawings can begin to give you ideas for separating layers ready for a multiple layered linocut print.

You may need to draw directly onto the sheet over your drawings or in between them – for example in ink or pen to outline a shape. Maybe write a few words over the top that reflect your topic and help to strengthen the mood you are looking for.

If you have the space, stick or pin up your idea sheets on the wall of where you are working. By constantly having the images and source material in front of you when working (instead of having to constantly flick through your sketchbooks), it can help to keep the creative process flowing and your prints inspired.

An example idea sheet including magazine cuttings, drawings, colour swatches, string and material samples. The theme here was fairies and the forest.

Studio Space

It is always a good idea to have a dedicated 'studio' space or area that you can use for your printmaking and to store your prints and materials. This does not need to be a large space or have expensive printing presses, plan chests or high specification equipment. A basic table space to work, area to store your materials and clean dry space to store prints is all that is needed.

You may find that you need to use a kitchen table, dining table, spare bedroom or if you are lucky you can convert a shed or garage into a studio. Or you may have access to a professional printmaking studio nearby that has all this and more!

The space that you will need to work in is broadly needed for four functions:

1. Preparation Area (Preparing Blocks)

This area / table will be needed for when cutting and preparing blocks. This will also include drawing and creating ideas and cutting out stencils. This can be the same area that you then use to print on later but you will need to make sure that it is cleaned up afterwards.

Basic requirements of this area will include:

Table – Must be sturdy so that it does not wobble when you are cutting or working, therefore disrupting your work. It must also be at a height comfortable for working at – not too low or too high. Many artists like to use a workbench instead of a desk to work at which will need to be higher than a table as you will be standing to work. Sometimes by standing up to cut your blocks, it can help give you added pressure down the cutting tool making it easier to cut.

Chair – If you sit down when working, you will need a chair or stool at a correct and comfortable height for you.

Good lighting – It is essential when cutting you have good light to see what you are working on and you are not straining your eyes. Sometimes having a small (daylight) lamp next to your working area when cutting a lino block can help.

Cutting Mat – You can also use a cutting mat to protect your table when working on a lino block instead of a bench hook. Place a tea-towel underneath it to help stop it slipping. Always use a cutting mat for cutting paper to protect your table.

Rubbish Bin – To throw away all the cut lino shavings, scrap paper and general rubbish you create

> ▶ **Susan's Tip…**
>
> "If you have the ability to plan out a full studio space (e.g. shed or garage), make a plan of the space first using graph paper to mark out where everything will go. You will then make the most of the area you have and fit all the required components of the studio in the most logical places."

Bench-hook – A bench-hook is a flat piece of board or wood with a strip of wood nailed to either end. One strip is on the underside to hook over the edge of the table and one is on the top to act as a barrier, stopping the lino from slipping when cutting. When cutting, you work away from you using the back of the bench hook to press against. This is often a useful item to avoid errors or cuts to your fingers! You can make a bench-hook yourself by simply attaching 2 strips of wood to a piece of MDF or you can purchase a pre-made one from good printmaking suppliers. The pre-made sort will often have strips of wood on 2 edges or even a triangle cut out of the back edge to allow the block to rest at a 45° angle as well. These can also be plastic as well as wooden.

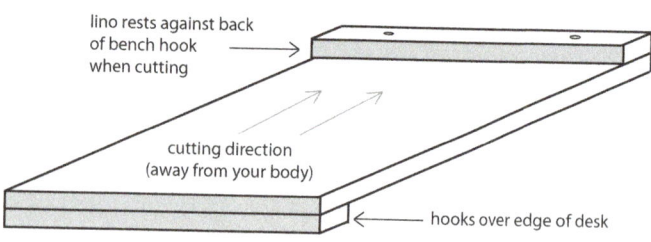

DIAGRAM OF A BENCH-HOOK

A BENCH-HOOK BEING USED TO CARVE A LINO BLOCK

2. The Printing Area

This area needs to be a clean, flat table space that you allocate for printing. The larger the area you have available to use for printing, the easier you will find it to work. More space will allow you to comfortably lay out all your materials, inks, rollers and paper without ink touching clean paper or having to pile things on top of each other.

A table such as a large kitchen table, dining table or even a kitchen work surface, works well for a printing area.

AN EXAMPLE PRINTING AREA

The diagram on the next page shows how to organise your table or work surface when working with lino. As you can see from the diagram, there are three main sections on the desk space. The first (left) is where your clean printing paper is stacked, the second is in the middle where the backing paper / registration sheet is placed, and the third (right) is where you roll out the printing ink on some perspex, glass or marble.

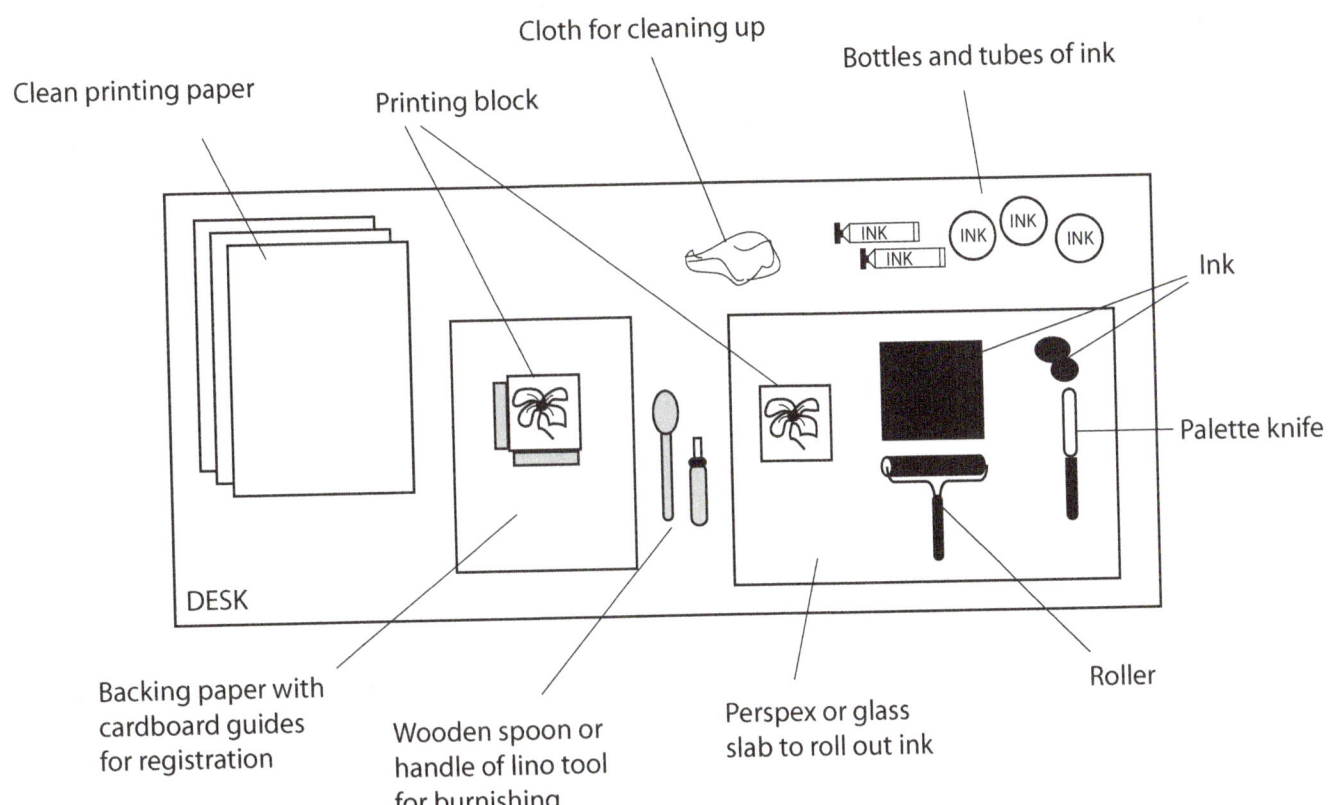

This layout can of course be varied and each printmaker will have a preference in the way that they work. However, by using this layout, your clean printing paper is always at a safe distance from the rolled out ink, keeping it clean. Once you have printed onto a sheet of the printing paper, it can be moved away to a warm flat environment or hung up to dry.

The sheet of perspex, glass or marble slab to the right is an essential part of this layout. It provides a smooth, clean surface to roll out the ink onto. This must always be clean and free of dust, lino shavings or water before you begin rolling out your ink. Some printmakers use small plastic trays but by having a large sheet of perspex or glass to work on that almost covers your whole desk, it is easy to clean up the whole area by wiping with a cloth afterwards and you don't have to worry about damaging your table with ink as the perspex or glass will completely cover it.

A glass or perspex sheet for rolling out your ink, can either be bought in a large sheet from a DIY shop or use the glass from an old picture frame or large clip-frame.

> ▶ **Susan's Tip...**
> "If you are using the same desk space to print and cut the block, make sure that you clean away all lino shavings so that they do not get caught up in your ink or stuck to your printing paper!"

It is also a good idea to put down a layer of newspaper or fabric (such as a sheet or blanket) over your desk or table before working to protect it, especially if this is your kitchen work surface or dining table. If the table is to be permanently used for your printmaking, use several sheets of newsprint paper and completely cover the table with it, securing the edges and joins with parcel tape.

Wherever you set up your table for printing make sure again that you have good light and ventilation. Sometimes by simply arranging your table in front of a window this can provide good light, good ventilation and a good view to inspire you!

Another good way to help you work, can be to stick up photographs, idea sheets or drawings on the walls in front of where you are working. Whether you do this in the area you prepare ideas and blocks or in this printing area is completely up to you.

It is also a good idea if possible, to visit an open access printmaking studio to see how a professional studio is laid out to give you ideas.

3. Storage Area

You will need somewhere to store your materials, tools and paper as well as wet and dry prints. When storing inks and other chemicals:

- The area you store materials in must be cool, dry and out of direct sunlight.
- The materials must be in a place where you will not knock them over.
- A series of shelves on the wall near where your printing area is, or in drawers of the desk you use to work can be ideal.
- Keep inks the right way up to prevent spilling.
- Always close the lids of tins and tubes of inks.

When storing tools such as lino cutters and rollers:

- Always make sure tools are dry before storing to prevent rusting.
- Keep cutting tools either in a specially dedicated stand, the box they came in or a roll-up cloth holder. Never throw them together in a pencil case or drawer as the blades will knock against each other and become damaged.
- Keep all tools in a safe way. In other words, put away or cover the blades of craft knives and lino cutters so that you do not cut your hands.
- If you can, try to hang up rollers rather than storing them together in a drawer or box. If the rubber of a roller is left on a flat surface for a long period, it will develop a flat line across it, damaging the surface. Most plastic and metal handled rollers have a hook or hole at the end to enable you to hang them up. If not, attach a small screw-eye or hook to the end.
- When storing lino (used and unused) keep it in a flat dry environment.

In an ideal world, a mixture of shelves and hooks for tools such as rollers and palette knives works the best. By hooking your tools on screws and then drawing around them with a pencil line, you can see at a glance where each tool is stored and can see when any are missing.

OCHRE PRINT STUDIO IN GUILDFORD, SURREY - ETCHING PRESSES

4. Drying Area (for drying prints)

It is important to allow your prints to dry in the correct way and in a safe place so that they do not become warped or damaged. The requirements for drying your prints are fairly simple as you will ususaly print onto dry rather than damp paper - a warm safe environment where your prints can safely be left for the time it takes them to dry. This can either be laid out on a flat surface or hung up.

If using a flat drying area:

- Make sure the area is flat, dry and warm.
- Make sure there is no water, ink or dirt that could damage your paper.
- This flat area could be a table, the floor, shelving unit or a (more expensive) drying rack.
- Make sure that the area is clean and free of dust, lino shavings or any other small bits and pieces that could get stuck to the ink.
- Make sure that the prints are away from your printing area to avoid wet ink and away from areas where you might tread on them.
- Make sure the prints are separated when you lay them out so that they do not stick to each other.
- Make sure it is not a windy environment, which could cause them to blow away.

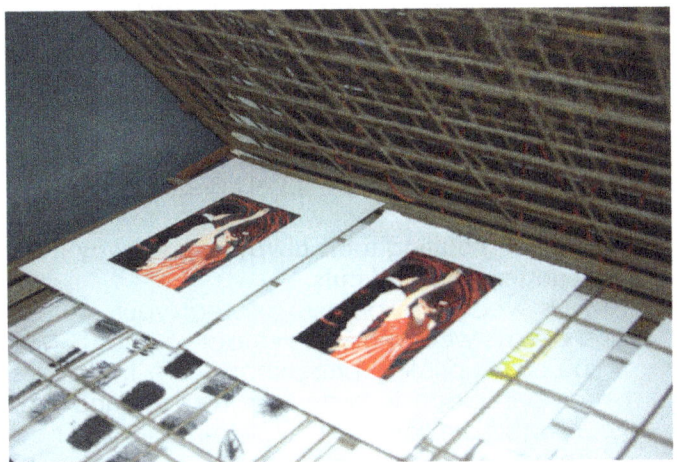

PRINTS DRYING IN A DEDICATED DRYING RACK

Hanging up your prints to dry:

Hanging up your prints to dry can be a very good way of assisting them in the drying process. It generally makes sure that they are out of the way of your printing area and will give you more space to work and print, without the likelihood of spilling ink on your freshly printed work.

There are several professional drying racks that you can buy for hanging prints but these can be costly and also impractical if you are working at home.

Think 'washing line'! There are several cheap washing lines designed for indoors and utility rooms that can double up as your method of drying or you may have one already. There are some great plastic fold away designs that allow you to fix one end of the line to one wall and then extend the other to a hook on another wall – these can go over baths or in utility rooms. They usually have 5-6 rows of string for hanging your prints on and fold away quite conveniently.

A SELECTION OF PRINTS DRYING INSIDE ON A HOME-MADE 'WASHING LINE'

You will need to use simple clothes pegs or bulldog clips to hang up your prints on the lines of string. Make sure that the pegs do not damage the paper as you hang them up. Wooden pegs tend to work best or clip an extra slip of paper between your printing paper and the peg to prevent dents.

The other benefit of hanging your prints up to dry is that they are fixed in place and will not blow away in a draft. To speed up the drying time, a fan heater can also be placed underneath the hanging prints.

When your prints are fully dry they can be stored away. When storing finished, dry prints:

- Make sure that all your finished prints are kept in a clean, dry environment out of direct sunlight.
- Keep finished editions in a folder or portfolio if you have little space.
- Make sure that your prints are never in an area where they could become damaged by water, printing ink or even pets or young children!
- Always interleave finished prints with acid-free tissue paper to protect them.
- Further details on presenting and storing finished prints is covered in **Chaper 4.**

In addition to these four areas, you will also need access to running water. This is mainly for cleaning your working area and washing tools. Try to keep water away from your printing paper and drying prints to avoid damage to the paper and your final prints.

▶ Health and Safety

It is always important to bear in mind certain health and safety issues such as ventilation and lighting when working.

- Make sure that wherever you work has good light (natural if possible) to stop your eyes from straining to see.
- When using any type of solvents or chemicals (including oil-based inks) make sure that you have good ventilation. Working in an area with a window, with an extractor fan or with an open door will help.
- Make sure that your working area (table) is at a height suitable to you, so that you are not bending over too much when working.
- Make sure that any tables you work on are steady and secure.
- Keep all sharp objects such as cutters in a secure and safe way (i.e. wrapped up or on hooks).
- If you start to use lots of oil-based inks, wear protective gloves or use a barrier cream on your hands to protect them.
- When using oil-based inks use household vegetable oil rather than solvents to clean up.
- Avoid getting solvents that you may use for cleaning up on your hands too often.
- Read all instructions on inks, chemicals, cutters etc before starting your work.
- **When using cutting tools always work away from your fingers to avoid cuts.**
- Always wear an apron to protect your clothes and always wear shoes to protect your feet.
- If you use a printing press, make sure that this is secured in place to a desk or the floor and that your fingers are kept well away from the print bed when printing.

Materials for Linocut Printing

There are a number of general materials as well as specialist materials and tools that you will need or are useful to have for carrying out linocutting. Below is a general list of many of the requirements that you will need. Some of them may only be occasionally used, some a lot and some are purely suggestions. Also, in the 'Tools and Materials' list for each 'Step-By-Step Guide' part of this book, specific materials required for each technique will be detailed.

- Selection of cutting tools for lino
- Lino blocks of various sizes and thicknesses
- Selection of pencils
- Eraser
- Thin and thick permanent marker pens
- Charcoal
- Selection of paintbrushes
- Apron
- Metal ruler
- Craft knife / scalpel or Stanley knife
- Cutting mat
- Pair of scissors
- Plastic or latex gloves
- Masking tape
- Sellotape
- Stack of old newspapers
- Selection of rags (old clothes) for cleaning
- Cellulose sponge for cleaning
- Cloths for cleaning
- Palette knife
- Roller(s) of various sizes

- Selection of printing inks (water and oil-based)
- Acid-free tissue paper
- Newsprint paper
- Cartridge paper of various sizes
- Printing paper
- Tracing or greaseproof paper
- Carbon paper
- Sandpaper
- Bucket or bowl for water
- Washing up liquid or soap
- Vegetable oil
- Sketchbook(s)
- Glue
- Perspex or glass for inking slab
- Sheets of thin acetate (clear plastic)
- Cardboard
- Wooden spoon, baren or other tool for burnishing
- Cocktail sticks
- Cotton wool
- Cotton buds
- Camera
- Relief press (optional)

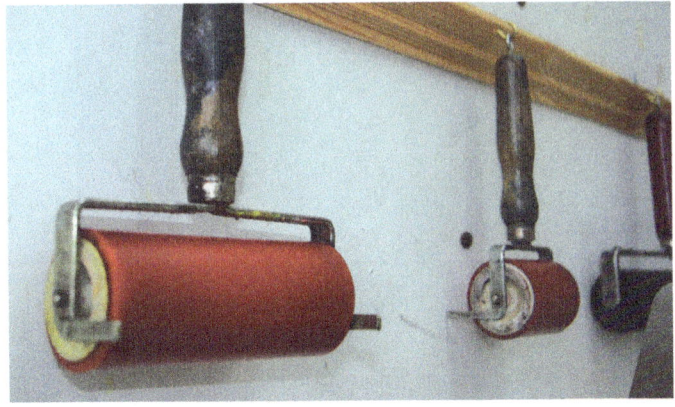

▶ Printing Inks

There are a wide variety of printing inks available for relief printmaking. The type or brand of ink that an artist chooses to use depends greatly on the type of work they carry out and their personal preference.

A ROLLER INKED WITH OIL-BASED INK

It is possible to produce basic prints or proofs using acrylic paints, gouache or watercolour but much better results are gained using special printmaking inks. They will also be easier to use and are specifically designed for use with these processes.

These inks can be loosely divided into two types: water-based and oil-based. Oil-based inks have traditionally been used by most printmakers in the West for many years for linocut, with water-based inks being a little further behind in their development. In the East, for example Japanese woodcut artists, have used water-based inks for centuries. However, more recently there has been a lot of development of ink technology and now there is a wide selection of good quality water-based inks with better quality finishes to choose from.

When buying inks for the first time, chose a small selection of essential colours to work with (e.g. black, white and primary colours). From these you can create a wide variety of colours to use by mixing different quantities of these basic colours together.

▶ Water-Based Inks

Water-based inks are those soluble with water and have certain advantages including that they are safe to use and can be cleaned up easily with water.

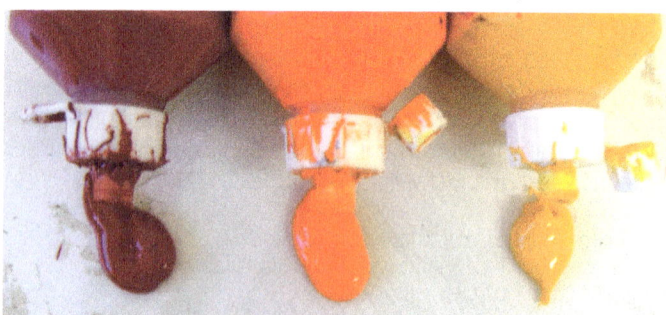

Water-based inks dry relatively quickly too, so that your prints can be ready within a matter of minutes – useful when you have limited time or space for prints to dry. Some water-based inks can dry to a waterproof finish.

On the flip side, this means that water-based inks can often dry on the printing slab when working, especially in hot weather and the tubes and tins of ink have a tendency to dry out faster than oil-based inks. Large areas of colour printed with water-based inks can also cause thin paper to warp or crinkle as the ink dries.

APPLYING BLACK OIL-BASED INK TO A ROLLER READY FOR PRINTING

▶ Oil-Based Inks

Oil-based inks are soluble in oil and are cleaned up with either vegetable oil (recommended) or a solvent such as white spirit. They can therefore stain hands and clothes much easier and are more difficult to clean up. When working with oil-based inks always ventilate your working area well and protect your hands as much as possible.

Oil-based inks take a lot longer to dry, so prints will usually take at least overnight to fully dry. This does however give them the advantage that you can spend a much longer time printing and preparing the block. The inks will not dry on your printing slab or from your tin of ink so quickly. They will also not cause paper to crinkle when drying (or wood blocks to swell if you use wood instead of lino).

Many printmakers tend to prefer oil-based inks for the quality of finish produced and the points above. Oil-based inks will often produce a better quality result, picking out any very fine, detailed cuts and producing a very smooth surface to the finished print.

However, there are now several brands of inks (e.g. Caligo Safe Wash Relief Inks) that are oil-based but washable with soap and water taking the best qualities of oil-based inks but also the ability to clean them up easily without the need for solvents.

▶ General Notes About Inks

It is worth trying both water-based and oil-based inks to make your own decision as to your preference and which complements your work the best. If you are new to linocut, we recommend that you start out using water-based inks (which are also generally cheaper) and progress to oil-based inks later on. This also saves investing in a large variety of different inks when starting out.

It may sound obvious but always look to purchase dedicated 'relief printing' inks for use with linocutting, rather than 'etching inks' which are for intaglio processes such as drypoint and etching.

As you develop your printing skill and become more familiar with linocut, you will become more familiar with the inks that you use. You may notice that some inks are very transparent when you use them and others very opaque. Also, some inks may be very quick to dry and others take a very long time.

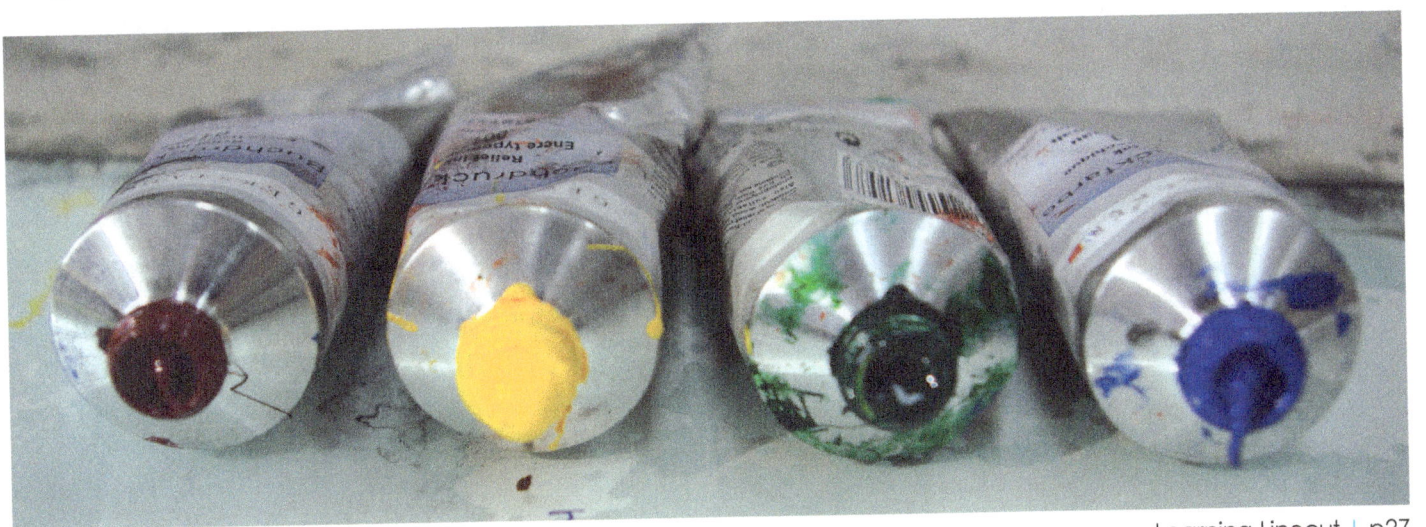

▶ Altering the Quality of Inks

Some inks (generally more expensive) contain a lot of pigment and some are generally thicker and more tacky than others. These different qualities will depend on the type and quality of ink that you purchase and you will begin to form a preference to different qualities in the inks you use.

Some of the qualities of oil-based (and some water-based) inks can be altered and enhanced to suit your printing needs by mixing various additives into the inks:

- **Retarders:** to slow down the drying time of the ink.
- **Thinning Oil:** to modify the viscosity of oil-based ink (usually linseed-based). Useful when an ink is very stiff when straight from the tin.
- **Extender:** is a colourless material that will increase the amount of ink without losing viscosity. This in effect will increase the transparency of the ink to make it more 'see-through.'
- **Cobalt or Manganese Driers:** for speeding up the drying time.
- **Anti-Dry Fluids:** For spraying onto rollers etc to stop drying.
- **Magnesium Carbonate or Talc:** to add stiffness to inks.
- **Wiping Compound/Tack Reducer:** to make wiping easier, reduce tack and improve ink transfer on difficult papers.
- **Gloss Finish:** To give the final print a 'shiny' finish.
- **Pearl Finish:** creating a 'pearl-effect' finish to the ink.

This gives you a great amount of control over your final linocut prints. Therefore experiment with mixing your ink colours or see what happens when one colour is printed on top of another. This is especially effective when using transparent inks. Where a second colour is layered over a first, an entirely new third colour can be produced. Some very effective results can be produced by the layering of thin, see-through colours over the top of each other.

Inks are usually obtained in small tubes or larger tins. We would recommend you start with smaller tubes of inks until you are confident with the technique, happy with the ink and sure that you will need more of it. Inks can also be very deceptive and last a long time as you only need a small amount rolled out very thinly to create a good quality print.

The only other consideration is how light-fast an ink is i.e. will the ink colour fade very quickly or last for many years.

INKING UP A SMALL LINO BLOCK USING LIGHT BLUE WATER-BASED INK

▶ Susan's Tip...

"When mixing up a new colour, always start with the lightest ink first and gradually add in smaller amounts of the darker ink(s) until you achieve the correct shade."

▶ Paper and Papermaking

Paper is made from plant fibres that are mashed together to create a pulp, which is then made into sheets. Along with ink, paper is a vital material needed in linocut printmaking – and you will use a lot of it! All the relief printing we discuss in this book is designed to be printed onto paper and not fabric, but feel free to investigate fabric printing as a way of developing your art.

As a general rule with printmaking, always choose smooth papers to print onto i.e. not papers that have a coarse texture to them such as most watercolour papers. Similarly, very shiny papers will also repel ink, making them very hard to work with.

The colour, texture and weight of a paper will greatly affect the final prints that you produce and there are such a wide variety of papers available for you to experiment with.

Paper is another material that is down to the individual artist's personal preference. The best advice we can give is to try a wide selection of papers as you progress to see what you like, what works for you and what does not. There are several factors that influence your paper choice:

- The colour of the ink you use.
- Whether you use water-based or oil-based ink.
- The size of your print.
- Whether you hand-burnish or use a press.

In particular, when relief printing by hand-burnishing, it is a lot harder to print on a very thick sheet of paper, as it tends to slip more when you burnish. Thin but strong papers are more preferable here.

Therefore in this section we will introduce some papers that you may want to try in your work.

▶ Newsprint & Cartridge Paper

To start with we recommend that you have a good stock of newsprint paper and cartridge paper. These standard papers are available in varying sizes, or in sketchbooks from your local art shop or printmaking supplier.

These affordable papers will allow you to experiment and try the techniques we introduce without spending a fortune. You can also think about using standard photocopier paper, which is again easy to obtain and relatively inexpensive.

You can use cartridge paper as your backing sheets for registration, for proofing a print, drawing on and for creating idea sheets.

Newsprint is generally thinner than cartridge paper and in addition to printing on, or using as padding, it is also good for drying surfaces and drawing on.

▶ Specialist Printmaking Paper

There are a wide variety of specialist printmaking papers available. Generally the higher quality the paper the longer the sheet will last and the better quality finish you will achieve.

Always try to look for acid-free or neutral PH papers as these will last longer and not turn brown with age.

Machine made and handmade papers are both available to use for printmaking and your art shop or paper supplier will be able to show you examples and suggest the best types of paper to try with the type of work you are producing.

Handmade papers are especially good for printmaking and although they are some of the most expensive, they can really produce a great end result. Handmade papers also have a 'deckled' edge from the frame that created the edges of the paper. This means that unlike machine made paper that has straight cut edges handmade papers have edges that are ragged.

Hot pressed papers are also very good types of paper to use for printmaking as they have smooth surfaces to work onto. Cold pressed papers are lighter general papers and rough papers have a lot of texture, which can be difficult to work with.

The way that a paper absorbs the ink is also important. With hand-printing and printing several colours on top of each other, paper that absorbs the ink well is an advantage. Unsized paper is more absorbent than sized. 'Sizing' refers to the way that paper sticks together. Unsized paper dissolves in water very easily and sized will tend to repel water more. Therefore a lightly sized paper will hold itself together well but allow good printing. Paper that is soaked before printing will need slightly stronger sizing to withstand the water.

Some examples to try include:

- Somerset
- Fabriano Bianco
- Zerkall (smooth)
- Arches
- BFK Rives

'THE LOOK-OUT BRANCH - HIMALAYAN PAPER' (LINOCUT WITH CHINE COLLE ON HANDMADE HIMALAYAN PAPER), LIZ TOOLE, 2009 - 51CM X 76CM

▶ Japanese Papers (Washi)

Japanese Papers (*Washi* – *wa* means Japanese and *shi* means paper) are an excellent selection of papers, made from the fibres of the bark of Japanese shrubs. They are usually expensive due to the processes involved in making them, but are strong and good at absorbing the ink. Many Japanese papers are almost tissue-like in their appearance but this gives them the added quality that you can see the ink appear through the paper as you burnish by hand. Examples of Japanese Papers to try include:

- China White
- Hodumura
- Tosa Washi
- Hoshu
- Shoji

▶ Papermaking

Making your own paper can be an excellent way to produce unusual and interesting quality papers to print onto. These will often have stronger textures than the papers you can buy, but you will have the ability to add materials and items into the paper or add your own watermark. It is also a good way to use up scrap paper.

▶ Tools and Materials

- 2 old buckets
- Selection of scrap paper
- Water
- Wallpaper paste
- PVA glue
- Old food blender
- Small mesh screen (similar to screen printing but with a low mesh count)
- Spatula or spoon to stir
- Paint to colour the paper if required
- Materials such as leaves, glitter, petals, thread to add to the paper

▶ Step-By-Step Guide

1. Start by tearing up the scrap paper into very small pieces no more than an inch square. Try not to use newspaper as this will make your paper grey in colour.

2. Put these scraps into a bucket and fill the bucket with water. Leave this to soak for at least 24 hours. This creates the paper pulp.

3. Using an old blender (or hand-whisk if you do not have a blender) place a small amount of the pulp in the blender and add more water (one part pulp to 4 parts water). Add a few drops of PVA glue or a small amount of wallpaper paste. If you want to add colour to the paper add some drops of poster paint.

4. Blend until completely smooth (the mixture should be like cold thin porridge) and place in the second bucket. Continue to blend all the rest of the pulp.

5. You can now begin to create your paper. Leaning over a bath or working outside gently pour or ladle the paper mixture over your mesh screen until you have an even covering to create a sheet of paper.

6. Shake the frame slightly to even out the pulp mixture over the mesh and let as much of the water drip out as possible. If you want to add items (e.g. glitter or leaves) into your paper add them now before the paper starts to dry. This sheet of paper in the screen can then be left to dry in a warm dry place. Drying outside can work well and it can also be sped up by using a fan heater. This drying process can take several days if the place you are working in is cold or the paper is particularly thick.

7. When dry, the paper can be carefully turned out of the mould. The side touching the mesh will be a lot smoother than the other side.

Papermaking is a messy but fun exercise and you can achieve some interesting and valuable qualities in your paper for printing onto.

▶ Linoleum

Linoleum (lino) is a composite sheet material (originally used for flooring) made from a mixture of powdered cork and linseed oil that has a hessian or burlap backing. The linoleum that printmakers use is specially prepared for the purposes of relief printing and usually comes in thicknesses such as 3mm or 5mm and is usually brown or grey in colour.

Printmaking suppliers will either supply the lino in rectangular blocks of different sizes or a large roll. Due to its flexible nature and thickness of just a few millimetres, these blocks and rolls can be cut to the desired size using a craft knife and metal ruler or even a pair of scissors if an unusual shape is required.

The surface of the lino is smooth and flat, making it a good material with which to begin relief printing. However, some lino can be relatively hard, especially in cold weather or when the lino becomes more brittle with age. To make the lino easier to cut it is often a good idea to warm it before cutting using a hairdryer or radiator to make it more flexible.

ABOVE: SOME LINOLEUM BLOCKS. BLOCKS CAN BE BOUGHT IN DIFFERENT COLOURS, THICKNESSES AND SIZES FROM SPECIALIST PRINTMAKING SUPPLIERS

▶ Linocutting Tools

There are several different V-shaped tools, gouges and knives that can be used to cut into the lino and each different tool will make a different mark. Some tools will make thin detailed lines and others are used to remove large areas of lino when flat white space is needed. Woodcut tools will also work with lino and all these tools can be purchased from most printmaking materials suppliers.

A LINOCUTTING TOOL IN USE

There are generally two different types of tool that you can use for linocut:

1. Lino cutting sets - consisting of a plastic or wooden handle with cheap replaceable blades that you throw away when blunt. This is a fairly inexpensive way to start and will allow you to get used to the different type of blades and gouges available.

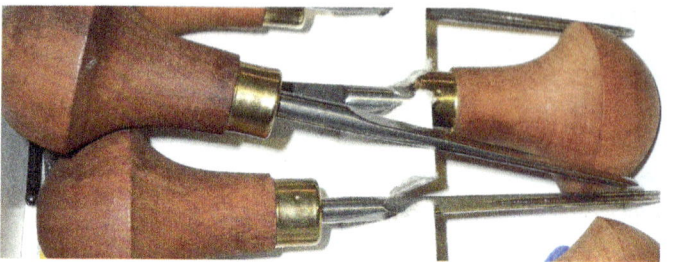

2. High quality linocut (or woodcut) tools - with a fixed wooden handle and blade that will last many years but require sharpening regularly to keep them sharp enough for cutting.

Whichever tools you use, make sure that they are stored properly in a clean dry place. Never throw them together in a drawer or pencil case as this will damage the metal blades. Some of the cutting sets come with boxes but you can also buy specially designed stands or carefully roll the tools up in a cloth holder. Choosing the appropriate cutting tools will make a big difference to the final image that you create.

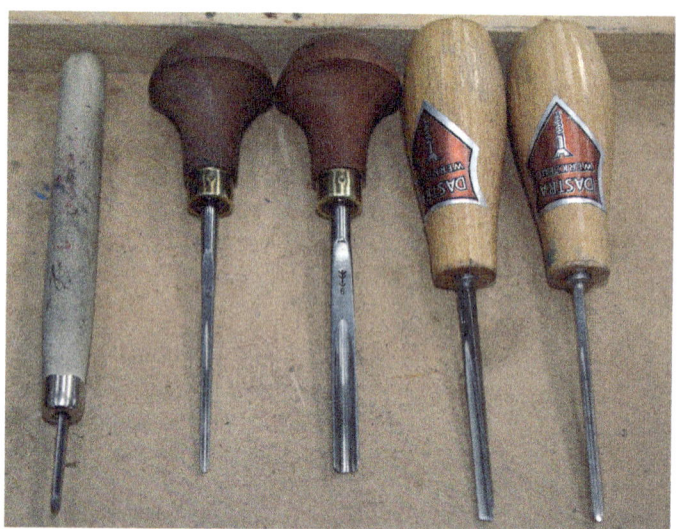

ABOVE: A SELECTION OF LINOCUTTING (OR WOODCUTTING) TOOLS OF DIFFERENT QUALITY AND MAKE - THESE ARE ALL TOOLS WITH FIXED ENDS THAT REQUIRE REGULAR SHARPENING. THEY SHOW SOME OF THE AVAILABLE 'U' OR 'V' SHAPED ENDS.
LEFT: WOODCUT TOOLS WITH 'MUSHROOM' SHAPED HANDLES THAT CAN ALSO BE USED FOR CUTTING INTO LINO. (NOTE: WOOD WILL BLUNT THE ENDS MORE THAN LINO WILL.)

▶ Susan's Tip...
"Always work with sharp tools to avoid tearing your lino or cutting your hands!"

Gouges - Gouges are tools with a rounded U-shaped end and are available in various sizes.

V Tools - As suggested by the name, these tools are V-shaped at the end and are available in various sizes to cut a sharp crisp 'V' into the plate. The very small v-tools are called veining tools and these are used for creating fine detail.

Knife - Another essential tool for cutting away lino is a sharp craft knife, scalpel or Stanley knife. A knife will allow you to cut very fine detail and thin lines and is for some printmakers the only tool that they use to cut their plate.

Profiles of Cutting Tools

Various 'V' Shape Cutting Tools

Various 'U' Shape Cutting Tools

A CUT LINO BLOCK - VINCE BRIDGMAN

'BEGINNING THE JOURNEY - TEA GREEN' (LINOCUT WITH CHINE COLLE ON CANSON MI TIENTES PAPER), LIZ TOOLE, 2010 - 46CM X 46CM

▶ Sharpening Your Tools

1. If you are using linocutting sets, when your blades are blunt simply throw them away and buy some new blades to replace the old. If however you invest in tools with fixed blades you will need to sharpen them regularly to keep them suitable for printing.

2. To do this you will need a water stone or oil stone. Water stones use water as a lubricant and oil stones use oil. These stones can be bought from printmaking suppliers where your cutting tools were bought.

3. The tool is sharpened by moving it back and forth on the stone with plenty of lubricant, keeping the blade at the same angle throughout to create a sharp edge for using. Rounded gouges will need to be sharpened using a rocking motion to create a sharp 'U' shape.

4. There is quite an art to blade sharpening, so a little practice and patience is needed.

Relief Press or Hand-Burnishing?

The process of printing is basically the transfer of ink from the plate or block onto the printing paper. Traditionally, printing presses are used to obtain strong and even pressure and achieve a good quality of detail in the final print. When at home or printing by hand this pressure needs to be created by simple easy to use methods. Therefore in this section we will discuss simple hand-printing methods for printing from a block or plate and in contrast, one or two of the different types of presses available.

▶ Hand-Burnishing Techniques

The process of rubbing the back of the printing paper to transfer the ink is called burnishing and all the methods we describe below are methods of hand-burnishing. Burnishing by hand can take a long time if your plate is very large but always work slowly and carefully. Make sure you keep the paper and block from slipping by always keeping one hand firmly on the paper. Thick printing paper will have a tendency to slip more than thinner paper so choose an appropriate paper with which to work.

We will run through the different hand-burnishing methods one by one:

'Rubber Stamp' - If you have a very small block it is easy enough to print the image by using it like a rubber stamp. Lay the printing paper face up on your desk and lower the block down on to it. Press the block firmly on the back to transfer the ink. Then lift up the lino to reveal the final print. You have the advantage with this method of seeing exactly where you place the block, making registration a lot easier.

Using your hand - This is a simple method and works well with plates that do not need a great amount of pressure. Lay the printing block **ink side up** on your desk and lay your printing paper over the top. Simply rub the back of the paper with the palm of your hand (or a folded up piece of soft cloth) to burnish. Always use the palm of your hand and not your fingers to hold down the paper, because you will be able to exert more pressure and your fingers may also leave an imprint. Work all around the back of the paper making sure to rub all the way up to the corners.

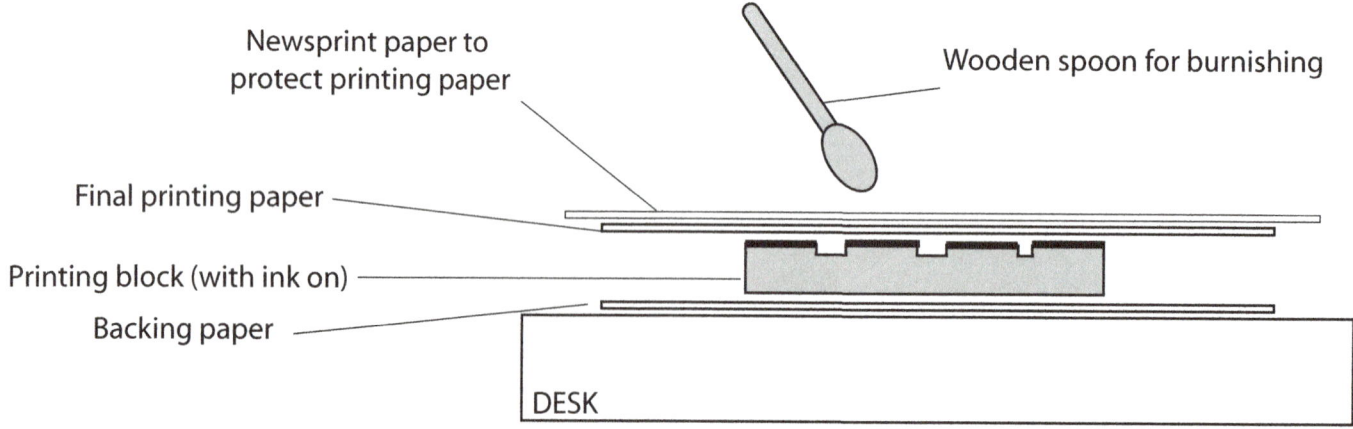

THE DIAGRAM ABOVE ILLUSTRATES THE USUAL LAYOUT THAT YOU WILL USE FOR BURNISHING WITH THE BLOCK INK SIDE UP AND THE PRINTING PAPER LAID OVER THE TOP.

Using a Wooden Spoon (or other tool) - Using a wooden spoon to burnish the back of the paper can be very effective. The smooth flat surface of the back of the spoon makes a nice even pressure on the paper. As before lay the plate ink side up on your desk and lay the printing paper face down over the top. Keeping one hand firmly on the paper to hold the block in place, begin to rub the back of the paper. Use a circular motion and work in a logical order around the back of the paper making sure to work right up to the edges of the block. To check your progress, lift the corner of the paper gently before finally lifting the paper to reveal the print.

Some people favour the wooden handles of linocutters for this purpose as they are smooth, easy to hold and readily available as you have just used them! But any tool that has a flat surface that you can rub on the back of the paper will work well. Using these methods, you may need to protect the back of the printing paper from the strong rubbing which may damage the paper. To do this, place a thin piece of cartridge or newsprint paper in between your printing paper and the tool you use.

BURNISHING A LINOCUT PRINT DURING A PRINTMAKING WORKSHOP

Using Foot Pressure - Using your foot can give a lot more pressure on the back of the printing paper and can work well with very large relief prints. Lay out the block **ink side up** with the printing paper on the top and then lay a sheet of newsprint over the top of this. Put a piece of board over the top to protect the paper and you can then use the pressure of whole body weight to print the image. Just make sure that you apply the pressure evenly and try not to let the paper slip.

Baren Printing - Using a baren to print is the traditional Japanese method of burnishing woodcut prints. A baren can be obtained from good printmaking suppliers and is a small round tool (usually about 13cm wide) and is made up of three layers. There is a coil of twisted bamboo laid over a laminated paper and this is covered on the outside with a bamboo sheath (leaf). The sheath is twisted at the back to form a handle. When using a baren you need to apply a drop or two of vegetable oil to the front flat part to keep it in good condition. The sheath will gradually wear over time but a new sheath or new baren can be purchased. Barens can also vary in price and a good quality tool that is very hard wearing can be fairly expensive.

IMAGE OF A JAPANESE BAREN

The baren is used in the same way as any other tool by rubbing on the back of the printing paper in a circular motion. It is particularly good for large prints as the coil of bamboo inside provides lots of areas of contact (unlike a wooden spoon which has just one point of contact) with the paper.

Using a Roller - Finally using the pressure of a larger hard roller on the back of the paper can also produce a good print. This is good for large prints or those that do not require a great deal of pressure. As the pressure is less than using a wooden spoon or other tool, slightly more ink may be needed to get a good quality print.

The Printing Press

Printing presses come in many shapes and forms and there are different presses suitable for the different techniques. The main purpose of a press is to allow printmakers to take even, good quality prints and apply the correct type of pressure for transferring ink from a plate or block onto the paper.

Presses can be very expensive but if you decide to specialise in linocut it can be worthwhile looking to invest in a press. A good quality press can last a lifetime so they are an investment worth considering seriously. They can also be very large and heavy, so you will need to have the appropriate space available to install it.

Different printmaking studios will have different presses available for use, so we would recommend trying the various presses within a professional studio with supervision first. We will briefly describe some of the types of presses available that are suitable for use with linocut:

▶ Etching Press

An etching press is designed for intaglio techniques and can be adapted to suit linocut as long as the block is not too thick. It has a metal bed that the plate and printing paper is placed onto. The bed is then passed through a roller or 2 rollers to exert strong pressure and force that paper down into the plate.

The bed is usually padded out with blankets and the presses come in different sizes, either free standing or for a table-top.

▶ Flat Bed Press or Relief Press

A flat bed press relies on direct pressure and is used specifically for relief printing methods. It has a large flat bed that the block with the paper on top is placed onto. A large platen (upper surface) is lowered down to force pressure directly onto the paper and the block. These presses are not generally used for intaglio techniques as they do not exert enough pressure.

ABOVE: A SMALL RELIEF PRESS (FLAT BED PRESS) BEING USED TO PRINT A LINOCUT PRINT
LEFT: A TABLE-TOP ETCHING PRESS

▶ Letter Press / Proofing Press

These old type-proofing presses (such as Adana Letterpress) can be also used to print relief blocks such as lino. They have a sunken bed that the old wooden type blocks used to be placed in. Lino that is the correct thickness can be printed using these presses. The paper is passed over the block by attaching it to a cylinder that passes over the sunken bed. Smaller proofing presses and letterpresses can be fairly affordable and easy to use at home.

Chapter 2: Linocut Basics

Chapter 2 will break down the basics of relief printing using linoleum step-by-step and look at how to produce a simple one-colour lino print. This information is essential in laying the groundwork for later chapters that will explore the technique in more detail.

We will start with preparing the block and how to hold and use the cutters, through to simple mark-making experiments essential for getting to grips with the technique. We then look in detail at image interpretation i.e. ways that you can transfer your image onto the block, ready for cutting. Finally, we explain the process of actually printing your lino block in one colour and how to register the paper.

'Autumn' (Linocut), Mike Johnson, 2010

'Gourds' (Linocut), Vince Bridgman, 2011

'Untitled' (Linocut), Susan Yeates, 2000 - 19cm x 34.5cm
DETAIL OF MY VERY FIRST LINOCUT PRODUCED WHILST AT UNIVERSITY.

Block Preparation and Basic Cutting

▶ Tools and Materials Required

- Linoleum blocks of various sizes
- Selection of lino cutting tools (v-tool, gouge etc)
- Stanley knife / craft knife
- Relief printing ink (water or oil-based)
- Palette knife
- Roller
- Glass slab / printing surface for rolling out ink
- Printing paper (smooth surface)
- Cartridge paper
- Roller / baren / wooden spoon for printing
- Pencil
- Masking tape
- Bench hook
- Plasters!

▶ Preparing the Block

1. Cut or purchase a piece of linoleum the size that you want your print to be. There are various colours and thicknesses of lino for you to choose from - 3mm thickness is generally student-quality lino and 5mm thickness lino is generally better artist-quality. A light grey piece may make it easier for you to see any drawn pencil lines but brown, green and dark grey coloured lino are all common.

For your first few prints, try small pieces of lino and simple designs until you are confident with the technique and can experiment with larger images. When you are first experimenting with linocut, your focus should be on learning the technique of cutting and printing correctly more than anything else.

If you are cutting a small block size from a larger sheet of lino (which is a more cost-effective way to purchase your lino), use a metal ruler, **sharp** craft knife and cutting mat.

Mark with a pencil on the surface of the lino the size that you want your final block to be. Then with the lino resting on the cutting mat and firmly held in position, gradually score along the line using a metal ruler and craft knife. Keep scoring until at least half-way through the lino block.

Pick up the lino and snap along the scored lines and finally cut through the hessian backing to detach your plate. If there are any stray pieces of hessian sticking out at the sides, cut these off too.

> ### ▶ Susan's Tip...
> "WATCH YOUR FINGERS WHEN CUTTING!! If you stick a strip of masking tape to the back of your metal ruler it will stop it slipping when cutting against it."

4. Using a pencil or some charcoal, draw your design onto the surface of the lino block. Don't forget that this needs to be a 'mirror image' because when you come to print you will turn the block over. Try not to use a material that will transfer when printing such as a biro or marker pen.

THE ORIGINAL PENCIL DRAWING THAT WLL BE USED - TAKEN FROM A SKETCHBOOK

2. Lino is usually prepared and sold ready to use, unlike woodblocks that may need a little more preparation before cutting.

Many artists however still chose to **rub the surface of the lino with a very fine sandpaper.** This serves to remove any small imperfections and provide a slightly more textured and absorbant surface for the printing ink to stick to.

In certain instances, artists will chose to mount their lino blocks onto a piece of wood to prevent the lino block from warping. This is helpful when printing a design that has lots of cutting away. Therefore because the lino is stuck flat to the woodblock, when you run the roller over it with ink on, it will not touch the cut away areas that might have been caught had the lino warped slightly at the edges. It is also helpful if you are printing the block using a press that requires a certain depth of block to work, such as a letterpress. Use a strong glue to stick the back of the lino to the woodblock and allow the glue to dry overnight and under pressure so that it sticks firmly and sand down the edges afterwards to prevent uneven edges.

3. After preparing your block and before cutting your design into the surface of the lino, it can be helpful to **slightly soften the block.** Warm the block gently by placing on a radiator or using a hairdryer. This will make cutting it easier especially in cold weather, if you have slightly blunt tools or if the block is old and a little tougher. Do this just before starting your cuts and marks.

DRAWING THE DESIGN ONTO THE LINO BLOCK WITH A PENCIL USING THE SKETCH AS A GUIDE

Learning Linocut | p39

▶ Basic Cutting

You can now start cutting your design out! Either place the lino on a non-slip surface or use a bench-hook to work against. Always make sure you have good light to see properly and try not to hunch over too much – choose a space and position that is comfortable for you.

CUTTING INTO A LINO BLOCK USING A BENCH-HOOK

A bench-hook is a flat piece of board or wood with a strip of wood nailed to either end. One strip is on the underside to hook over the edge of the table and one is on the top to act as a barrier, stopping the lino from slipping when cutting. When cutting, you work away from you using the back of the bench-hook to press against. This often helps to avoid errors where the block slips away from you or cuts to your hands. It also stops the cutting process being too straining on your hands, arms, neck and back.

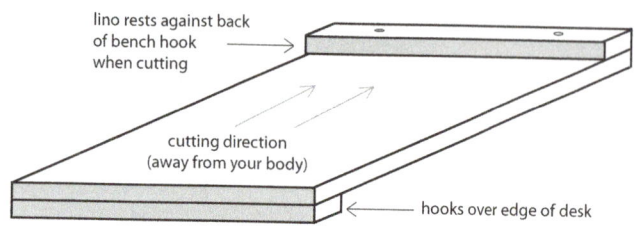

DIAGRAM OF BENCH-HOOK

CUTTING INTO THE LINO BLOCK USING A LINICUTTER (NOT USING A BENCH-HOOK)

If you are not using a bench-hook try using a tea-towel or another non-slip surface underneath your lino block to rest on.

Begin by using a small v-tool to cut out the basic elements of your design (e.g. a 1mm veining tool). Many people will cut around their outlines first to mark out the most important elements before then 'filling out' the design and removing the rest of the redundant lino.

Then use a gouge or selection of gouges (larger 2-4mm U-shape tools) for removing wider areas. When cutting into the block **always cut away from your fingers and body** resting the lino against the bench-hook if you have one. Hold the block with your other hand to stop it from slipping.

But don't worry if you do nick your fingers with a cutter – unfortunately this is all part of the learning process and even the most accomplished artists can end up with cuts to their fingers – that is what the plasters on the 'Tools and Materials' list are for.

▶ How to Hold a Linocutter

Hold the linocutter like you would a fork (or a door handle). The wooden or plastic handle needs to rest in the palm of your hand so that you can apply pressure down the cutter, using the full force of your arm. Hold the metal of the tool with your thumb and forefinger and a centimeter or two from the end of the cutter for extra control.

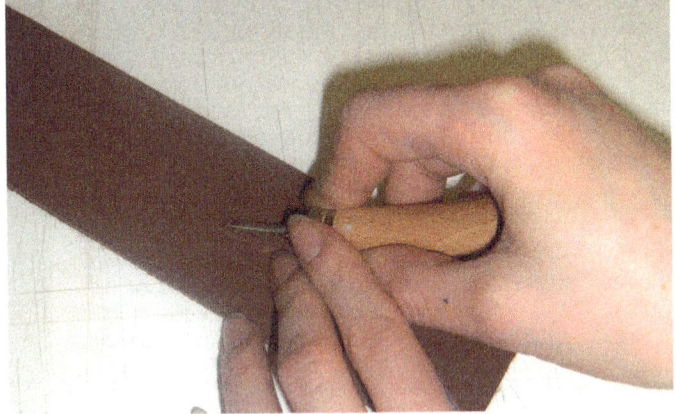

HOLDING A LINOCUTTER

CUTTING INTO THE LINO - NOTE THAT ALL FINGERS ARE BEHIND THE CUTTING BLADE!

When cutting, the tool should be at about a 45° angle to the lino block, directed away from you and away from your other hand holding the block.

Always cut away from you and try to cut in small smooth strokes rather than 'wiggling' the tool to get through the lino or trying to achieve one very long line at once. Smaller strokes leave less chance of error and you can build up your design gradually. You will probably find that smaller tools will appear easier to use as they have to cut through a smaller amount of lino compared to thicker tools.

Do not try to cut too deeply to start with. You can always cut out more but you cannot put it back! As a general rule, cut no deeper than about halfway into the block and certainly you shouldn't go as far as the hessian backing.

Do not forget that the areas you cut out will not print (i.e. are the paper colour) in the final print. The part that is left in relief (that you have not cut) is what you will ink up and is what will print. Therefore all you need to do is cut deep enough into the block so that when ink is rolled onto the surface of the relief (the non-cut area), the area that you have cut will not be touched by the ink.

To cut in a different direction simply turn the block around rather than directing the cutter back at you.

Some of the best results are those using bold, broad designs, without any fine detail. Fine, detailed lines are also a lot harder to cut with precision than broad designs and can prove harder to ink as well. You can always develop your cutting skill and try finer cuts as you get more experienced.

When you have finished cutting, rub out all the pencil marks from the surface and remove any loose pieces of lino that may have gathered in and around your cuts. Use a toothbrush or firm paintbrush to get into the deep areas of the block. The block should be clean, smooth and dry ready for printing...

▶ Susan's Cutting Tips

"We will quickly look at several tips on cutting into the linoblock to help you to make good quality cuts that will last the process of inking, printing and cleaning without deteriorating the lino."

TIP 1: As mentioned in the 'basic cutting' section, always take small shallow cuts first and then work further into them.

TIP 2: Cut no further than about half-way into the lino and definitely not as far as the hessian backing. If you cut too deep, firstly you are making it hard work and secondly it will make your lino very flimsy.

TIP 3: When cutting away areas of lino, always cut away from your design i.e. away from your small 'outlining' cuts and out towards the edge of the block. If you work towards your design you risk the cutter slipping and cutting through something you don't want it to. If you always work outwards from the centre to the edge of the lino, if you do slip, the cutter will simply skid off the edge of the lino rather than into your design.

TIP 4: When cutting away large areas of lino use large cutting (U-shape gouges) tools to save time.

TIP 5: When cutting around your design, your cuts should always slope down and outwards to give strength underneath the surface of the lino. In other words, the cuts shouldn't be at right angles to the lino or even cutting away under the surface of the lino. If you end up cutting away underneath the edge of your design you risk the edges breaking away and crumbling when placed under the pressure of printing. See the diagram below for examples of good and bad cutting techniques.

TIP 6: Think about the direction in which you cut away the lino. When you remove a large flat area of the block, the ink may still pick up small details and if you have carefully been cutting away in a certain direction it can add an atmosphere or flow to your image even though there is very little of the block remaining.

TIP 7: Always proof your image before deciding that it is 'finished'. You can always cut away further but you cannot put the lino back.

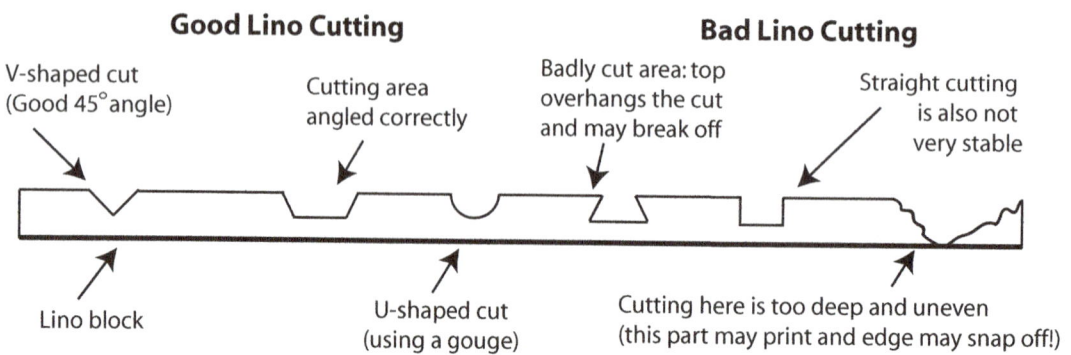

Good Lino Cutting
- V-shaped cut (Good 45° angle)
- Cutting area angled correctly
- Lino block
- U-shaped cut (using a gouge)

Bad Lino Cutting
- Badly cut area: top overhangs the cut and may break off
- Straight cutting is also not very stable
- Cutting here is too deep and uneven (this part may print and edge may snap off!)

Mark-Making

It is important to explore the type of marks that can be made using the cutting tools that we described in **Chapter 1**. The way the tools are used and the contrast of marks placed next to each other within just one print can produce very different results. By experimenting with different types of marks in the lino, your prints will become more accomplished, demonstrating a greater variation in final print.

As you become more familiar with relief printing, you will build up a style of your own and a way of working that suits the subject matter that you are tackling.

The image to the right is an example of some different marks that can be made using different V-tools, knives and gouges:

1. The marks at the top were created using a fine V-tool. Dashes and cross-hatching has been experimented with.
2. The marks here were made using a 1mm veining tool. (small 1mm gouge)
3. A 3mm U-shaped gouge was used for these marks.
4. These sharp marks and shapes were created using a craft knife.

A MARK-MAKING SAMPLER FROM A RECENT WORKSHOP

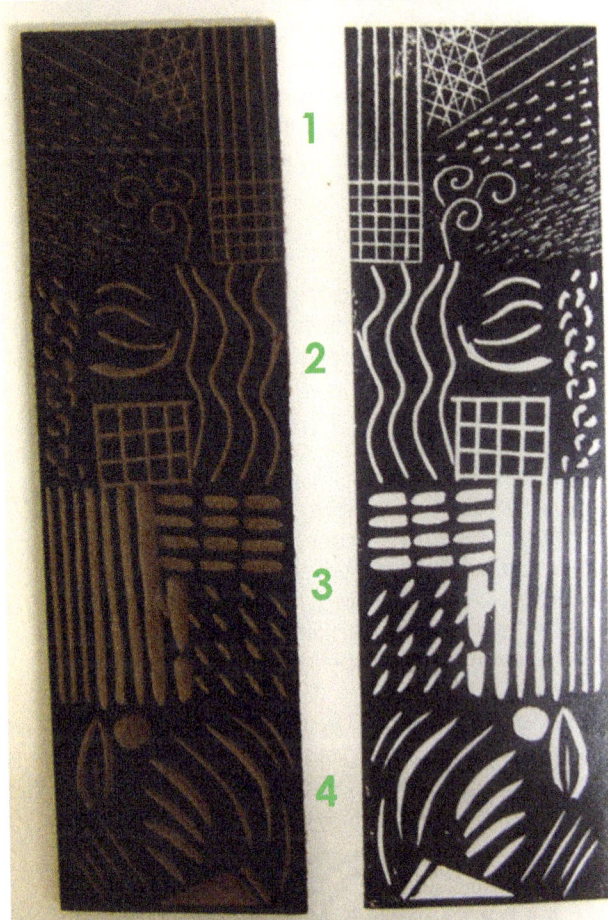

THE PHOTOGRAPH ABOVE SHOWS A MARK-MAKING EXERCISE IN LINO – THE INKED LINO (LEFT) NEXT TO THE PRINTED IMAGE (RIGHT)

> ▶ **Susan's Tip...**
> "I nearly always use this mark-making exercise when introducing linocut to a new group of students. Within a few short hours of starting printmaking you can have an attractive-looking print that gives you experience of the tools and the process. I have even seen students frame these samplers and hang them up at home!"

Learning Linocut | p43

▶ Your Mark-Making Sampler

Try the following exercise to produce your own mark-making sampler. Make sure that you have a selection of V-tools, gouges and a craft knife available to use.

▶ Step-By-Step Guide

1. Use a 8cm x 16cm square of lino and divide the block into 8 even sections each 4cm x 4cm by marking the lino with a pencil (2 squares wide by 4 high).

2. In each section, create a series of different marks and textures. Use each of the different tools you have available in turn and even try experimenting with other tools. (e.g. the sharp point of a needle). Try to make each section as different as possible – create dots, stripes, cross hatching, large gouges, small spirals etc. Refer to the mark-making diagrams on these few pages for examples of the marks you can make.

3. Print the lino in black water-based ink. Clean the lino up and then print again in black oil-based ink. By doing this you can see the differences in print quality from one type of ink to the other.

MARK-MAKING SAMPLER CREATED USING VARIOUS LINOCUT TOOLS. THE RESULT IS A SELECTION OF PATTERNS, TONES AND BACKGROUNDS THAT COULD BE USED IN YOUR PRINTS.

EXAMPLE MARK-MAKING SAMPLER EXPERIMENTING WITH TEXT AND BACKGROUND TEXTURES

4. By completing this 'sampler' you now have a simple linoprint demonstrating your cutting ability. It will act as a reference guide for when you are looking to make a certain type of mark in future prints. It gives you a great visual record of what different patterns, textures and general marks that each tool you own creates. Write down on one of the prints exactly how the marks were made, to remind you later on.

▶ More Cutting Suggestions

Text – When cutting out text into your lino block be very careful that you cut the letters as if they were a mirror image. It can help you greatly to use the carbon paper technique to help transfer the letters onto the block back to front so that when printed they are the right way around.

'My St Albans' (Linocut), Mike Johson, 2010
This black and white linocut has incorporated text into the imagery

Small Circles – To create small even circles in the lino, pick a U-shaped cutter that has a cutting end the diameter of the circle you wish to create. With the cutter almost at a 90° angle to the lino, cut into the lino twisting the cutter in a full 360° rotation as you do so. This will remove a small round piece of lino from your block – almost an exact circle!

Knife Cutting – Many printmakers use a knife or scalpel to produce relief prints and the knife is the essential tool for Japanese woodcut printing. To cut a block using a knife, you need to make 2 cuts into the lino to carve out a 'V' for each mark you make. Firstly make a cut in the lino roughly at a 45° angle. Then make a second cut to create the V at a 45° angle in the other direction so that the tip of your 2 cuts meet. You can then remove the 'V' of lino from the block to reveal your line. Using a knife can give you a very sharp point to your cuts into the block (see diagram to right.)

'Wiggling' – This can be a good technique for creating a certain 'torn' quality to your lines. In the print below this technique was used to create the effect of a ploughed field. As you cut into the lino, gradually rock the cutter from side to side to create uneven, torn sides to your cuts.

'Salisbury Fields' (Linocut), Susan Yeates, 2007- 20cm x 20cm

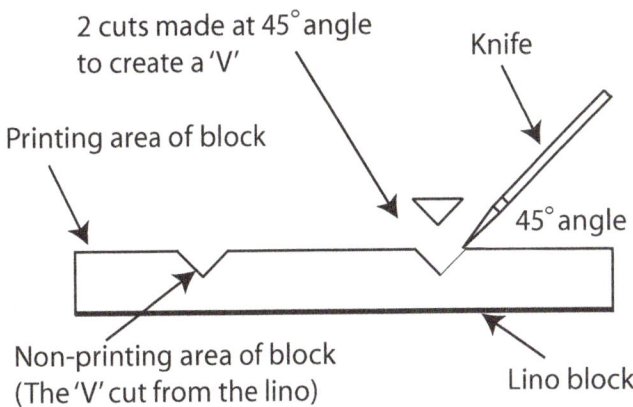

Learning Linocut | p45

◯ Image Interpretation

One of the hardest things to overcome for the novice printmaker (or even the most experienced at times) is the way in which an idea or image is interpreted and finally printed by the lino technique.

In particular, the simple transfer of an image from sketch, photo or thought to the cutting stages can halt even the most creative of minds for a moment. In the extreme, some artists are even put-off by the 'technical' aspect of printmaking believing that it is too far protracted from the initial creative idea or phase. However, others relish the 'art' and skill involved in the technique and just as a painter needs to become adept at their painting technique, so does the printmaker.

Relief printing works in a mirror-image and negative way so that unlike a simple pencil drawing which is very direct, it can often be hard to visualise or see the final image before the printing paper is eventually lifted and the print is revealed. But this is often the most interesting and exhilarating part of the printmaking process and many a successful print has been created by what can be termed the 'happy accident' (i.e. where an error in printing can end up producing an effect that you decide to use).

With time and as you become more experienced with the technique, many artists pick up either a style or a general sense for how they will interpret their idea or image without the need to think quite so much.

Some printmakers are very 'free' in their image creation, choosing to simply cut blind into the lino with no guidelines at all or even no image as a reference to work from. Other printmakers are slightly more prepared maybe working from a pre-prepared drawing or sketch that they play with or develop as they cut. And there are other printmakers who like to be absolutely prepared to the smallest detail and line within the print.

'ASSANA' (LINOCUT), SUSAN YEATES, 2009 - 20.5CM x 30CM

However you chose to work is completely up to you and there is no right or wrong way. In this book we will simply make some suggestions for ways that you could try that have been successful for other artists.

Do bear in mind that the more complex the final print, the more planning and preparation is required. If you are aiming to create a 6-colour lino print this will need accurate planning to make sure the colours match, register and produce the exact result that you want.

▶ Negative and Positive Cutting

Negative or positive cutting refers to the way that a shape or drawing is cut from the lino block. The easiest way to demonstrate this is to show a very simple shape cut in both a negative and a positive way. We will also look at cutting simple lines too.

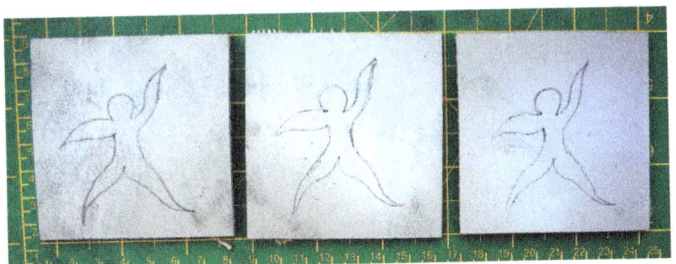

THREE SMALL LINO BLOCKS EACH WITH THE SAME INITIAL DRAWING MADE ONTO THE SURFACE BY USING A PENCIL.

In the image above, the same shape was drawn onto three small lino blocks using a pencil. Each block was then treated (and cut) in a different way to deomonstrate the three ways that you can interpret an image: negative cutting, positive cutting and cutting simple lines.

THE SAME THREE LINO BLOCKS WITH CUTTING MADE INTO THEM. THE LEFT HAND SIDE HAS NEGATIVE CUTTING, THE MIDDLE HAS POSITIVE CUTTING AND THE RIGHT HAS LINES CUT OUT.

▶ Susan's Tip...

"Always think carefully about how to treat a design for relief print and whether you are going to cut in a negative or positive way – or incorporate both!"

The three ways that the same image has been cut out in the lino are:

1. On the left side the drawing has been cut in a **negative way** – i.e. the area within the pencil was cut out from the lino producing a white shape on a black background.

2. In the middle, the lino has been cut in **a positive way** – i.e. the lino around the drawing was cut away leaving a black shape on a white background.

3. On the right side **only the pencil lines of the shape itself were cut out** i.e. the line was cut directly out from the lino producing a white line with a black background around and inside the line.

NEGATIVE AND POSITIVE DEMONSTRATION - THE LEFT SIDE HAS BEEN CUT IN A NEGATIVE WAY, THE MIDDLE IN A POSITIVE WAY AND THE RIGHT BY CUTTING OUT THE LINES ONLY.

Therefore from this demonstration you can see that even with the simplest of shapes there is more than one way to interpret this for a final print. Once you have transferred an image onto the surface of the lino, think carefully about which areas you wish to cut out and which you wish to remain. There may be areas of negative cutting, areas of positive or you may create your entire print using lines only.

Often when starting out, the temptation is to only cut out the pencil lines and it takes practice to implement negative and positive cutting effectively.

Now try your own negative and positive cutting exercise using a simple design of your choice on to three small blocks to experiment with the ways of translating a design in lino.

Looking at the Background and Creating Tone

When planning a design, many printmakers spend a great deal of time considering the way that a background is created. This also applies to areas in your design that are a half-tone i.e. an area that is somewhere between a solid block of ink and a completely cut-away white area. Therefore printmakers often use a series of dots, lines or even cross-hatching to create these effects.

Your mark-making exercise will have helped you with creating a series of marks that you can use for this specific purpose. Take a look at the small mark-making samplers on the previous page and some of the example works here and throughout the book for interesting suggestions for how a carefully cut background can enhance a print.

'ABOS' (LINOCUT), RICHENDA COURT, 2010 - 64CM x 48CM

'BROADSTAIRS CATCH' (LINOCUT), ANDY JOHNSON, 2010 - 45CM x 45CM
NOTE: LOOK AT HOW AN INTERESTING TEXTURE HAS BEEN CREATED WITHIN THE SKY AREA BY THE WAY THAT THE LINO HAS BEEN CUT INTO.

> ### ▶ Susan's Tip...
> "When planning a new print, always experiment with various different options for the background to see what compliments your basic design the best and creates the exact type of atmosphere that you are trying to create."

▶ Repeat Pattern

In addition to using one piece of lino to create a print, many artists instead use smaller lino blocks printed several times to create much larger patterns (a repeat pattern). This is often seen in work involving textiles and can require careful planning. Try looking at various fabrics to see if you can spot different repeat patterns in use.

When experimenting with repeating a pattern, try out your designs onto cartridge paper first and try it in different colours such as contrasted colours, different shades of one and layering colours too.

▶ Repeat Pattern Structures

There are various different structures that you can use to repeat a small block. Here are some suggestions for you to try. With all these patterns, the blocks can either be placed directly next to each other or with gaps in between. You can also combine different sized blocks or rotate the blocks within the patterns.

1. Straight repeated rows

2. Mirror image

3. Half-drop design (block shifts down)

4. Brick repeat (block shifts left or right)

5. Diagonal repeat

6. Clusters of shapes

Learning Linocut | p49

▶ Direct Transfer from Sketch to Print

This method is one of the simplest ways of transferring your drawing or design onto the block.

▶ Tools and Materials

- Lino block
- Sharp pencil or biro
- Tracing paper
- Carbon paper
- Sketch or drawing
- Masking tape
- Piece of thin white cartridge paper

▶ Step-By-Step Guide

1. Cut a piece of lino the same size as your original sketch or drawing.

2. Cut a piece of tracing paper, thin white cartridge paper and carbon paper all the same size as your original sketch or drawing.

3. Place the tracing paper over your drawing and tack in place with some masking tape.

4. Draw around your design with a pencil or biro onto the tracing paper, including all the important elements that you wish to include in your lino print.

5. Remove the tracing from the sketch and turn it over so that the drawing is on the underside of the piece of tracing paper.

6. With the lino in front of you, place the carbon paper on top (carbon-side touching the surface of the lino), some thin white paper on top of this and the back-to-front tracing on top of this. Use some masking tape to tack it all in place. The white paper is included to allow you to see the drawn lines on the tracing paper. Then using a sharp pencil or biro **firmly** draw over the lines of your tracing.

7. When complete, take off the tracing, carbon paper and white paper to reveal your drawing on the lino. This image will be the mirror image of your original sketch. This means when printed it will be the same way around.

8. If you need to make the lines a little stronger go over them with a pencil. If you are working on a dark-colour lino, using a white pencil may make the lines stand out more.

9. Once you have made your cuts into the lino based upon your tracing, rub out all the pencil or carbon lines and you are ready to print!

TRANSFERRING THE IMAGE FROM A PIECE OF TRACING PAPER ONTO THE LINO BLOCK USING BLACK CARBON PAPER

▶ Other Suggestions

- If you have created an image or edited a photo in a software package on your PC, create a mirror-image of your design, print this out onto paper and then draw over this directly with carbon paper underneath.

- If you are confident with your drawing ability you can place your sketch in front of you and draw from it free-hand onto the lino using a pencil. This often gives a more 'natural' finish that reflects the fact that the lines drawn onto the lino were drawn freely.

- Why not try using a permanent marker pen instead of pencil to make your marks. Find a pen that will remain fixed to the surface of the lino when printing. i.e. not transfer onto your final print or wipe off when cleaning. This is very helpful for the 'reduction' technique in particular.

PREPARATORY SKETCHES BY ARTIST MAX ANGUS USED TO CREATE THE **3**-COLOUR LINOCUT BELOW

'THE HARVEST HARE' (**3** BLOCK LINOCUT), MAX ANGUS - 34CM x 24.5CM

● One-Colour Printing

▶ Step-By-Step Guide

1. When you are happy with the cuts you have made into the lino you are ready to start printing. In this step-by-step guide we will take you through the process of printing a lino block in one-colour. Black is a good colour to start with as it has the ability to create good contrast between the lightest and darkest areas.

2. Before printing, make sure that you have rubbed out all pencil or charcoal marks from the surface of the lino. Your desk and printing area must also be clean and free of dust or pieces of lino that could get into the printing ink. See **Chapter 1** for details of how to layout your printing area.

3. If you are using oil-based ink, it is helpful to use latex gloves to protect your hands during this part of the process. It is also helpful to wear an apron and cover any areas in your workspace that you do not want to get covered in ink.

4. Prepare several sheets of printing paper all the same size and a piece of cartridge paper as a backing sheet to print from. As this is a one-colour print we do not need to worry too much about 'registration' at this stage (see end of the chapter for details).

5. Squeeze out a small amount of your printing ink onto the printing surface and spread this out into a line using a palette knife.

> ### ▶ Susan's Tip...
> *"For oil-based inks try soaking the paper to make it damp for printing and therefore more receptive to the ink. Leave the paper in cold water for 5-10 minutes and then blot thoroughly before using. This is only suitable for one-colour prints."*

Learning Linocut | p51

SQUEEZING OUT SOME PRINTING INK ONTO THE PRINTING SURFACE

6. Choose a roller just slightly larger than your lino block. Roll it over the ink until the ink is spread into a thin layer giving the roller a nice even coverage. You do not need to press the roller down very hard to pick up the ink – simply allow it to roll back and forth over the ink. You can change the direction of the roller as you roll and sometimes pick the roller up completely from the ink and start rolling in a different place.

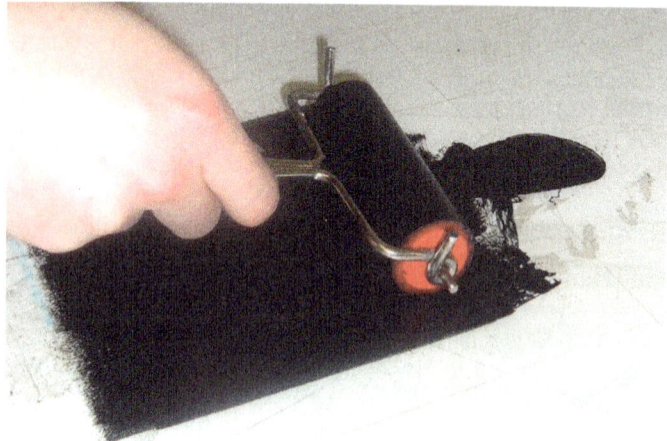

ROLLING OUT THE INK INTO A THIN LAYER - TO COVER THE ROLLER IN INK

7. You do not need to roll out all of the ink that you have put out onto the printing surface. All you need is enough to give the roller an even coverage. The ink rolled on the printing surface and transferred onto the roller should not have a heavy texture i.e. be too thick – the ink should be smooth and even.

TRANSFERRING THE INK FROM THE ROLLER TO THE LINO BLOCK

8. Once the roller is evenly covered, roll the roller over the surface of your lino block several times and in different directions to evenly cover the block with ink. You only need gentle pressure when rolling and gradually build up your ink coating on the lino. If you use too much ink the fine detail of your print will be flooded by the ink, too little ink and the print will be faint when printing. Make sure that you roll right up to the edges of the block so that no areas are missed. If you are using oil-based ink you can really take your time with this to make sure that the ink is perfect. Try not to get ink on to the back of your lino block as well.

COVERING THE LINO BLOCK COMPLETELY WITH PRINTING INK

p52 | Learning Linocut

9. Once your block is inked correctly, carefully place the lino block in the centre of your cartridge paper backing sheet, **ink side up**. It helps if you mark out where to place the block first with a pencil to centralise the print. This piece of cartridge paper will give you nice clean edges around your print. (Some printmakers choose to always take off their gloves when handling paper to keep the paper clean and only handle the inking part with gloves on.)

This will transfer the ink onto the paper from the lino block. Always work in a circular motion, pressing firmly but not allowing the paper to slip. Make sure that you cover the whole of the print and watch out for the edges, which are easy to miss! Often standing up whilst doing this will give you better pressure onto the paper as well.

LOWERING THE PRINTING PAPER DOWN ONTO THE INKED LINO BLOCK

PLACING THE INKED BLOCK IN THE CENTRE OF A CLEAN BACKING SHEET

10. Gently lower the first sheet of your printing paper, good-side down over the top of your lino (which is ink-side up), lining the paper up with the backing sheet.

11. Carefully press the printing paper down onto the ink using the palm of your hand. If your printing paper is very thin, place a piece of newsprint or scrap paper on top of this so that you do not damage the printing paper.

12. Then firmly holding the paper in place with one hand so that it does not slip, use a roller, wooden spoon or baren to rub (burnish) the back of the paper.

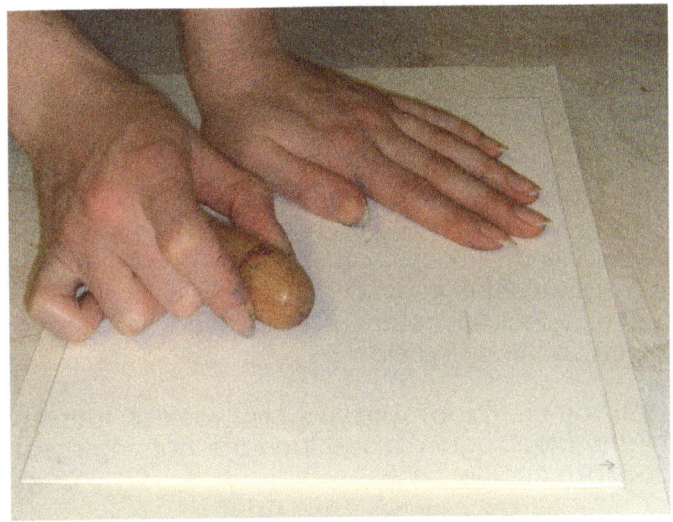
BURNISHING THE BACK OF THE PAPER BY HAND (USING THE HANDLE OF A LINOCUTTER)

Learning Linocut | p53

13. Alternatively, if you have access to a printing press, place the lino with its backing paper and printing paper, padded by newsprint or blankets into the press as per the instructions of the press.

14. After burnishing thoroughly (or putting through the press), check whether the ink has transferred properly by peeling back one corner of the paper. If the image has not transferred across properly, replace the paper and carry on burnishing. Do not remove a large area of the printing paper when you place it back down again because it may not line up causing a blurred edge and therefore misprinting.

LIFTING UP THE PRINTING PAPER TO REVEAL THE FINISHED PRINT

15. When the print is complete, gently lift up the printing paper to reveal your print. Leave the print to dry in a warm flat environment. Either place the print in a drying rack or leave on a flat surface. If you are in a rush, a small fan heater or hairdryer can be used to speed up the drying process.

16. If you are happy with your print you can then re-ink the block again, place it on the backing sheet and take another print.

17. If you feel that the print needs more work, clean

THE FINISHED PRINT - A SIMPLE ONE-COLOUR LINOPRINT

the plate thoroughly, allow it to dry and start to cut out more lino as necessary. This method of printing one print to check it is called **proofing**. It is a good habit to get into to check your progress and see the result before printing onto high quality printing paper.

18. Print 6-10 copies of your print. Notice that these prints are all identical (or nearly identical as there will be subtle differences in each print you produce). This is called an edition of prints.

19. When you have finished printing, clear up your printing area. If you are using water-based ink, wipe off the ink from the plate using a damp cloth. **Do not simply run the block under a tap**. If you get the hessian backing of the lino wet it will cause the lino block to bend as it dries making it very hard to print from in the future. If by accident you get the hessian backing of your lino block wet, dry the lino as much as you can with kitchen towel. Then place it between 2 or 3 sheets of kitchen towel, surrounded by newspaper and then weight it under several heavy books and leave over night to dry. This pressure will keep the block flat as it dries and stop it bending. For oil-based inks use vegetable oil and white spirit to clean up (see **Chapter 4** for further details).

○ Registration

Registration is the process by which a printmaker will line up more than one colour or block within a print so that all colours register exactly in the right place on top of each other. This means that before starting printing your first lino block, you need to decide which method to use so that the print is successful.

There are lots of different methods for doing this and we will discuss a few simple methods here that you can use when printing linocut prints of more than one colour. Each printmaker will have their own preference for the way they work and register a print, but as long as it works and the colours all line-up in the final print then the method is successful!

It is good practice to get into the habit of using some form of registration even when you are printing a one-colour print. This means that your print will be lined up in the exact place on each piece of printing paper. It also allows you the flexibility to add a second colour should you want to after printing the first.

'ROOFERS' (LINOCUT), ANTHONY DYSON, 2006 - 61CM x 46CM
ARTISTS PROOF ON JAPANESE PAPER

REGISTERING THE FINAL COLOUR OF A LINOCUT AT A PRINTMAKING WORKSHOP
TO SEE FINAL PRINT SEE P73 - (SUE MOLLOY)

> ### ▶ Susan's Tip...
> *"For all of the registration methods that we describe, it is always a good idea to mark the back of each sheet of printing paper and the back of each lino block with an arrow to indicate which edge is the top."*

Learning Linocut | p55

▶ Simple Registration

This is one of my favourite methods for registration with linocut and one that I teach a lot in live classes and workshops. It requires very little complicated thought or specialist equipment and is simple to prepare.

Take your time when making the registration board - use a pencil and ruler to accurately measure the paper, board and positioning of the block. This will prevent errors and make it more likely that your colours will line up.

▶ Step-By-Step Guide

1. Prepare several sheets of printing paper - make sure that your sheets are **exactly the same size**. In particular make sure that the left and bottom edges are at right angles to each other. If the paper has a deckled edge use the deckled edges for the top and right hand side and trim the left and bottom edge so you have a sharp edge to your paper.

2. Then place one sheet of your printing paper in the middle of a larger cardboard backing sheet. Draw around this sheet accurately using a pencil. Then stick some small pieces of card, fixed with masking tape or PVA glue at the left and bottom edges of your paper. These act as guides along which the paper rests in place.

3. Remove the printing paper and place the lino block that you are using in the middle of the cartridge paper (so that it sits in the middle of where your printing paper would be). If necessary use a ruler to mark out accurately the centre.

4. Draw around the block with a pencil and ruler and then fix small thin pieces of card alongside the edges of the block. Therefore when you place your block into its correct position you are resting it against the cardboard markers each time so that the position is accurate. This will work even when your block is an unusual shape.

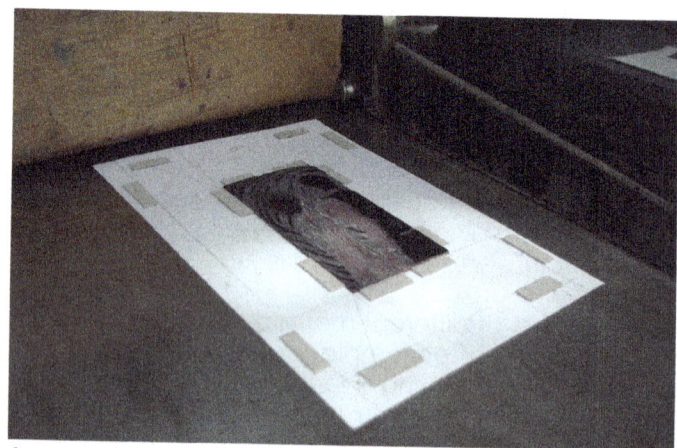

A LINO BLOCK ON A REGISTRATION BOARD READY FOR THE PAPER TO BE PLACED ON TOP

5. This method will mean that when you place your block and paper in their marked spaces each time, the ink will print in the same place and your print will be properly registered. Always use the same two edges of the paper to aid registration. i.e. the left and bottom edges of the paper and the lino block to lower them into position in line with your registration pencil marks.

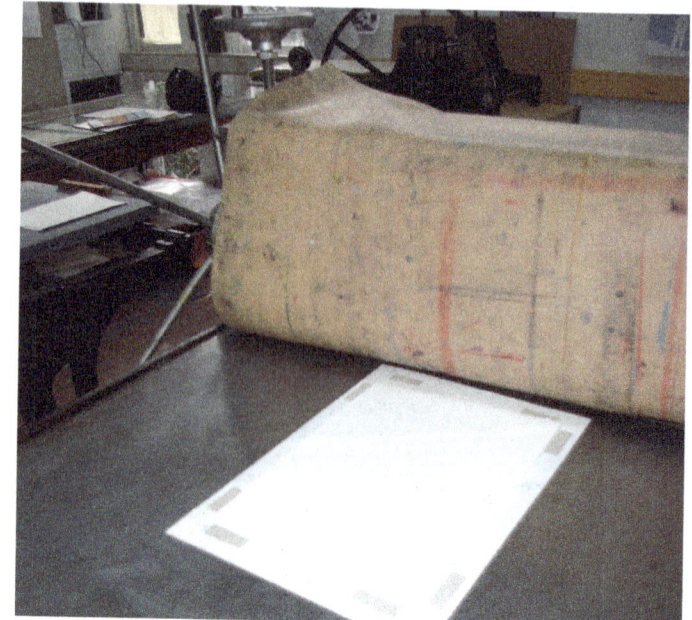

THE PAPER PLACED OVER THE TOP OF THE LINO - READY FOR PUTTING THROUGH THE PRESS

▶ 'Cheats' Registration

This method I call the 'cheats' registration as it mainly relies on the eye and steady hand of the printmaker and does not follow the traditional methods used by printmakers lining up relief blocks. This method should really be used as a last resort in registration and is prone to error. However, it can be a great way of recovering a print where the registration has gone wrong or for those who simply find the other methods too tricky or time-consuming.

▶ Step-By-Step Guide

1. Print the whole edition of your print in the first colour onto separate sheets of paper without using a registration method. Leave these to dry and prepare a block for the second colour.

2. Once your block is inked with the second colour, lay out on your working space one of your prints that has the first colour on it face-up.

3. Carefully lower the inked block **ink side down** onto the paper, lining up the edges of the block with the edges of the first colour. This can take a little patience to get it in place but once there, press gently on the back so that the ink touches the surface of the paper.

LOWERING THE INKED SECOND BLOCK DOWN ONTO THE PRINTED FIRST COLOUR (RED) — THIS IS THEN TURNED OVER SO THAT THE PAPER IS ON THE TOP READY FOR BURNISHING

'MATTHEW', WHITSTABLE (LINOCUT), ANDY JOHNSON, 2010 - 45CM x 15CM

4. Steadily then lift and turn over the paper with the block stuck to it – slide one hand underneath and one on top and slowly turn the two over without letting the block slip. You can then burnish as normal and your second colour will be lined up over the top of the first.

5. If you are using a press there is no need to turn the paper and block over – simply place the printing paper with the block on top directly into the press, padded with newsprint paper on either side.

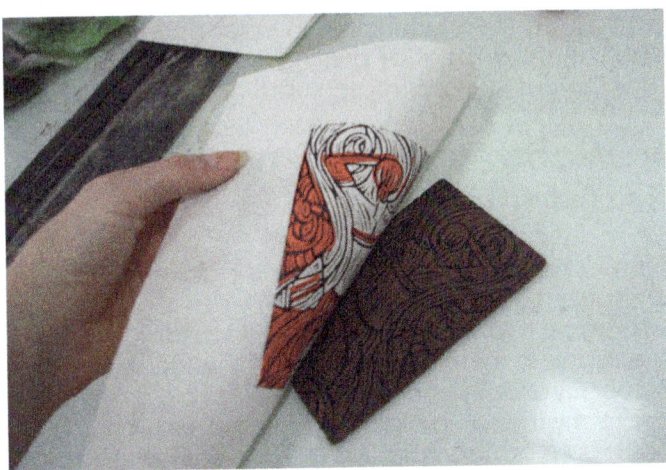

LIFTING UP THE PRINTING PAPER FROM THE SECOND BLOCK (BLACK) TO REVEAL THE PRINT

This is by no means a perfect method for registration and very hard if the edges of the block are cut away a lot, if the block is very large or you have a print that requires very accurate registration. However, with a steady hand (and maybe a quick pencil mark around the first colour to help define the edges) it can be a quick and useful method of registration.

▶ Cut Triangles

This method is very similar to the simple registration method.

1. Prepare a piece of cartridge paper or cardboard as a backing sheet and several pieces of printing paper – all exactly the same size. On the backing sheet, mark in the centre the outline of your block using a pencil.

2. Laying one (or more sheets) of the printing paper over the top of the backing sheet and holding firmly in place so that they don't slip, cut 2 small triangles into the sides of the card and paper. Keep doing this until all your pieces of printing paper have triangles cut into them that match with the backing sheet.

3. Before printing, tape down your backing sheet to your printing area or the press bed. Each time you print place the block face-up inside the pencil lines and line up a sheet of printing paper face-down so that the cut triangles match up.

▶ Wooden Dowels or Registration Pins

Some printmakers will prepare a backing board of chipboard or MDF to print from. At the top of this they will place two metal pins or wooden dowels. Holes are made in the printing paper at the top so that the paper fits exactly over the dowels. The block is placed in exactly the same place each time marked in place using card or wood pieces. The paper is lowered onto the plate whilst slotted over the dowels. These holes can be cut off the final print and do not forget that the paper may need to be slightly larger to start with to allow for the holes.

This method is not transferable to a printing press and is only suitable for hand printing.

'LOOK TO THE LIGHT' (LINOCUT), MARY BRANSON, 2010 - 86CM x 60CM
2-LAYER LINOCUT - EDITION OF 15

NOTE FROM THE ARTIST: THIS IS A ROMANIAN NEOLITHIC GODDESS WHICH I HAVE ADAPTED AND TRIED TO CREATE A POWERFUL AND TIMELESS COMPOSITION FOR HER TO EXIST WITHIN.

Chapter 3: Advanced Techniques

The first two chapters of this book examined the basic techniques for generating ideas for prints, discussed the materials you need and the methods for taking these ideas from lino block to the final print.

In this chapter we will develop further those skills, looking at more advanced techniques including multiple-colour linocuts using both the reduction technique and multiple block systems such as the key-block system.

Finally, at the end of the chapter we will provide a selection of other suggestions for you to experiment with, including alternative inking techniques, incorporating other printmaking methods and experimenting with other materials for the block itself.

ABOVE: 'RED TRACTOR' (LINOCUT), ANTHONY DYSON, 2006 - 61CM x 46CM
LEFT: 'THE WESTWAY' (REDUCTION LINOCUT), TOBIAS HILL, 2008 - 82CM x 120CM

Learning Linocut

Reduction Technique - 'The Suicide Print'

This technique involves 'reducing' a block to create a multiple coloured print. What this actually means is that one piece of lino is used, cut as normal to produce a first colour, then the block is 'reduced' i.e. cut into further and then this is printed over the top of the first colour. The plate can then be further reduced and printed again as your design demands.

The reduction technique is a great way to produce a multiple coloured print from just one block. One advantage is that the plate will always register well - i.e. the design of the second colour will always fall in line with the first due to the fact that the same block has been used. The disadvantage is that once you have reduced the plate you can't get it back again and re-print the first colour. Hence it is sometimes termed the suicide print! Due to the nature of the process, it is essential to print enough copies of your first colour to work with for your subsequent colours.

'SALISBURY FIELDS' (REDUCTION LINOCUT), SUSAN YEATES, 2007 - 9CM x 10CM

▶ **General principles to bear in mind:**

- When printing more than one colour using the reduction technique it is often a good idea to start with the lightest colour first and gradually print darker colours over the top, finishing with the darkest colour or black.

- Imagine that your first colour will almost be a background colour, your middle colour the highlights or colouring and the top colour the fine detail of the design.

- Try not to 'over think' and worry about the end result too much. Often you need to try the technique to really understand how it works. Print your first colour as normal from the lino block and then simply cut out some more of the block and print it over the top. As long as your design looks good when you cut it from the block, more often than not it will also look good when printed over your first colour.

- Start with a simple, straight-forward design on a small block following the step-by-step guide. You can then try more colours and larger blocks as you become more confident and experienced in the technique.

- When thinking about printing more than one colour, you need to plan for losing 1-2 prints in registration of each colour. i.e. if you are printing 3 colours and want 10 good finished prints you will need to start with about 14-16 of your first colour in case you lose 1-2 prints when you register the second and third colours.

In the demonstration we will look at a 3-colour reduction to explain the basic principles of the reduction technique.

▶ Tools and Materials

- Linoleum for the block
- Bench hook (optional)
- Cutting tools e.g. v-tools or gouges
- Printing ink
- Palette knife
- Craft knife / Stanley knife / scalpel
- Roller
- Glass slab / other surface for rolling out ink
- Printing paper (smooth surface)
- Baren / wooden spoon / other item for printing or press
- Pencil
- Paintbrush
- Materials for registration (e.g. card)
- Masking tape

▶ Step-by-Step Guide

1. Purchase or cut a piece of lino the size that you want your print to be.

2. Using a pencil or the carbon paper method, draw your basic design onto the surface of the block. Don't forget that this needs to be a 'mirror image' because when you come to print you will turn the block over. What you are doing here is drawing out the design, from which you will cut the first colour.

Some artists will go over these pencil lines with a permanent marker pen (one that will not print or rub off in cleaning). This will keep the lines in place as a guide for each colour of the reduction rather than having to redraw them each time.

3. Place the block on a steady surface ready to cut, or use a bench hook to lean against. Begin slowly cutting out the basic elements of your design using your cutting tools or a knife. You are cutting away the areas that will not print and be the colour of your paper (usually white) in the final print. The areas that you will leave uncut will print as your first colour.

TRANSFERRING THE DESIGN ONTO THE LINO USING CARBON PAPER

CUTTING INTO THE LINO FOR THE FIRST COLOUR OF THE REDUCTION

Learning Linocut | p61

When cutting into the block, always cut away from your body and keep your fingers behind the cutting blade. See **Chapter 2** for help on cutting your design.

4. Do not forget that what you are cutting will not be your final print – another colour will go on top so don't cut so much out that you have nothing left to reduce for your second colour.

5. When you are happy with your block, you are ready to print your first colour. If you are cutting and printing in one working area, throw away all the lino shavings that you cut from the block to leave a clean dust-free surface to work from.

6. Prepare several sheets of printing paper all the same size and a sheet of cartridge backing paper slightly larger. A smooth surfaced paper is always the best to use. Then prepare the printing area for simple registration as per the instructions in **Chapter 2**. Make sure that you have enough pieces of paper to produce your entire edition plus an extra 2 sheets per colour that you print. For example, if you are producing an edition of 20 of a 3-colour print, you will need to cut at least 26 pieces of paper to allow for wastage in the registration process or errors in printing.

7. Using a palette knife, place your first ink colour onto the glass slab or inking surface. As a general rule, when you start out, use a light colour for your first colour and gradually get darker for the following colours. Roll the roller over the ink until the ink is spread evenly into a thin layer.

8. Then roll the roller over your block several times and in different directions to evenly cover the block with ink.

9. Once you have covered the block with ink, place your block in the marked area of the registration board ink side up ready to print.

10. Carefully place your printing paper over the top, lining it up with the pencil marks and cardboard guides. Gently press the paper down onto the block using the palm of your hand so the paper has good contact with the ink. Always use the same two edges to place the paper next to your registration pencil marks or cardboard guides (left and bottom edges).

FIRST COLOUR OF THE REDUCTION PRINT - YELLOW

11. Firmly holding the paper in place with one hand, use a wooden spoon or baren to rub (burnish) the back of the paper. Press firmly and work in a circular motion, making sure not to miss the edges of the paper or let the paper slip. Check your progress and see whether the ink has transferred properly by peeling back one corner of the paper. Alternatively put the block and printing paper through a press.

12. When the burnishing or printing is complete, remove the paper to reveal the first colour of the print.

13. Then re-ink the block to print your first colour as many times as you need using all of the sheets of your printing paper you have prepared. Leave all the prints to dry in a warm flat environment. You must always make sure your first colour is properly dry before printing another colour over the top.

14. When you have completed printing your first colour, wipe clean your block with a damp cloth (for water-based inks) to remove all the printing ink and leave to dry. Keep the registration board for your simple registration system in a safe place as you will need this later on.

15. Find your original design and re-trace this onto the block again or re-draw by hand the areas that you want to cut for your second colour. You can also work freely without further pencil marks, using the cuts already in the block as your guide.

16. To start with, work with a slightly darker colour as your second until you are confident enough with the technique and how different colours work together.

17. When you have planned the second colour, cut out the lino from the block exactly as you did before, using the cutting tools.

18. When your cuts are made and you are happy with the design you are ready to print your second colour.

19. Ink up the block as normal using your second colour.

20. Print the block onto a plain sheet of paper first to proof it and check it is printing correctly.

21. When you are happy with it, place the inked block in the centre of your marked guide sheet as per the simple registration.

INKING UP THE SECOND REDUCTION IN BLUE. THIS IS THE SAME PIECE OF LINO THAT WAS USED FOR THE FIRST COLOUR, JUST WITH FURTHER CUTS INTO IT.

LOWERING THE PRINTED FIRST COLOUR DOWN ONTO THE BLOCK WITH THE SECOND INK ON

22. Then place one of your first colour prints over the top using the pencil marks and cardboard guides to register the paper in exactly the right place. Use the same edges as before to register the paper i.e. the left and bottom.

Learning Linocut | p63

THE REDUCTION PRINT - SHOWING THE FIRST AND SECOND COLOURS PRINTED

26. Once this second colour is printed, simply clean the block again, redraw the design and cut further into the block.

INKING THE BLOCK AFTER THE THIRD SET OF CUTS HAVE BEEN MADE USING BLACK INK. NOTICE THAT LESS OF THE LINO BLOCK IS LEFT TO INK UP COMPARED TO THE FIRST COLOUR

LIFTING THE FINAL PRINT UP FROM THE THIRD COLOUR

23. Burnish the back of the paper as usual to take the print or put it through a press.

24. Lift the paper to reveal your print with the first two colours printed.

25. Continue to re-ink the block and print all of your prints until your edition is complete. Leave them all to dry in a warm flat environment.

27. When this third set of cuts is complete, re-ink in a third colour and print over the top of your first two colours. This method will work with as many reductions as you want – why not try it with 4 or 5 colours?

THE FINAL REDUCTION PRINT SHOWING ALL THREE COLOURS (YELLOW, BLUE AND BLACK).

NOTICE HOW THE THREE COLOURS LINE UP AND HOW THE PRINT WAS STARTED WITH THE LIGHTEST OF THE THREE INKS AND THEN WORKED TO THE DARKEST.

▶ **Susan's Tip...**
"If your registration is not working properly, use the 'Cheats' Registration as described in Chapter 2."

'CAMDEN LOCK' (REDUCTION LINO PRINT), TOBIAS HILL, 2002 - 133CM X 90CM

NOTE FROM THE ARTIST:
"THE BLUE / PURPLE COLOUR OF THE WATER WAS ROLLED DIRECTLY ONTO EACH PRINT WITH AN UNDERINKED ROLLER TO GIVE A SENSE OF FOCUS TO THE CANAL AND REFLECT THE COLOUR FROM THE SKY. THIS WASN'T ORIGINALLY PLANNED IN THE CUTTING / PRINTING PROCESS BUT WAS A DECISION THAT I THOUGHT WAS REQUIRED TO ENABLE THE PRINT TO BE READ AS I INTENDED. HOPEFULLY THIS ILLUSTRATES THAT THE REDUCTION PROCESS ISN'T TOTALLY RIGID AND IT IS POSSIBLE TO MODIFY AN IMAGE."

Learning Linocut

Multiple Plate Printing - Key-Block

In this section we will explain and demonstrate how to produce a multiple coloured relief print using more than one block. In contrast to the reduction technique that uses one block that is cut into further for all the colours, separate blocks are used here for each colour. This means that the print can therefore be proofed and developed until it is exactly how you want it before printing the final edition of prints. It can also be re-printed at a later date if more are needed as the blocks can be kept and re-used.

There are several methods and techniques for planning out an image and preparing the plates. In this step-by-step guide, we will look at the 'key-block' system for planning an image. We will demonstrate a 3-colour relief print using 3 separate lino blocks.

▶ Tools and Materials

- 3 pieces of linoleum for the block
- Bench hook (optional)
- Cutting tools e.g. v-tool or gouge
- Printing ink
- Palette knife
- Craft knife / Stanley knife / scalpel
- Roller
- Glass slab / other surface for rolling out ink
- Printing paper (smooth surface)
- Baren / wooden spoon / other item for printing or a printing press
- Pencil
- Sandpaper
- Paintbrush
- Acetate sheets / tracing paper the same size as your block

▶ Step-by-Step Guide

1. Purchase or cut three pieces of lino the size that you want your print to be. Make sure that they are exactly the same size.

2. Prepare a design ready to use for your relief print where three colours can be printed. The design needs to be the same size as your lino blocks.

THE INITIAL PENCIL SKETCH FOR THIS 3-COLOUR PRINT - NOTE THAT SOME SAMPLES OF INK HAVE BEEN PLACED ON THE PAGE ALONGSIDE THE SKETCH

3. You will be using black as the final colour and two other lighter colours. It is the black block that is used to create the 'key-block' and this is the first colour that you prepare and cut but the last to print. This key-block is the detail of the print – the black drawing lines that define the image of your print.

By cutting this block first it gives you the detail of your print from which you can then plan where your other colours will be placed.

4. To help you plan your image, make a colour drawing or painting of how you want your print to look. Also experiment with the three colours next to each other using a little of your printing ink scraped thinly onto paper. Take your time to choose the correct colours that will work with and complement your planned design.

5. To prepare the 'key-block' trace your design for the black lines / detail onto a sheet of tracing paper. Then turn this over and place over your first block with a sheet of carbon paper underneath. Draw over the pencil lines to transfer your image onto the block. It will appear back-to-front on the block, but when you print it will be the same way round as your original drawing. You can also draw the design directly onto the block if you wish.

CUTTING THE KEY-BLOCK

6. When your design is transferred onto the block, cut out the design using your cutting tools, using your traced drawing as a guide.

7. When you have finished cutting, your 'key-block' is ready to proof.

INKING THE KEY-BLOCK READY TO TRANSFER TO THE OTHER TWO BLOCKS

8. Ink up the block using black ink. Print the image onto a sheet of cartridge paper to check you are happy with it.

9. Ink the key-block again and lower a sheet of acetate onto the block that is exactly the same size. You may need to use slightly more ink than with normal printing, to allow the ink to transfer from the key-block to the other blocks.

Learning Linocut | p67

APPLYING A SHEET OF ACETATE TO THE INKED KEY-BLOCK

10. **Whilst still wet**, lift the acetate from the key-block and lay the sheet of acetate over one of your other blocks, lining up the edges accurately. Press firmly on the back to transfer the black ink across. Lift up the acetate and leave the block to dry.

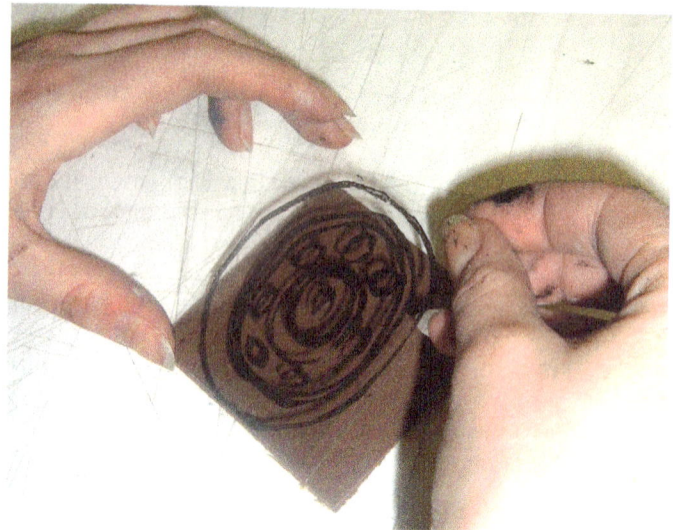

PLACING THE INKED ACETATE ONTO A BLANK LINO BLOCK

THE KEY-BLOCK NEXT TO A SECOND BLOCK WITH THE INK ON IT READY FOR CUTTING

11. Ink the plate again and repeat the process for the remaining block, again leaving it to dry before cutting. Wipe clean your key-block and leave aside for printing later. **This key-block is printed last over the top of your other two colours.**

12. You now have the image from the first block printed onto the other two blocks to aid you in cutting the second and third colours.

CUTTING INTO ONE OF THE OTHER BLOCKS (THE TRANSFERRED INK WAS USED AS A GUIDE)

13. Using the key-block and your sketch as a guide, cut out your second and third colours from the two blocks referring to your proof of the key-block and the original design for help.

14. Whilst cutting you can always print a proof of the other blocks to check progress.

A PRINT OF THE KEY-BLOCK (BLACK INK) PRINTED ON ITS OWN

15. When you are happy with the cutting and proofing of each block, you are ready to start printing your edition.

16. Prepare several sheets of printing paper ready for your prints. Make sure that you have enough to cover any problems in registration (i.e. always count on loosing 1-2 prints in the registration of each colour) and that all the sheets are **exactly the same size**. With prints of more than one colour you will always need to use dry paper rather than damp.

17. Prepare whichever registration technique you intend to use (see **Chapter 2**).

18. Print your first colour (e.g. the lightest colour) from one of your blocks, printing onto each sheet of printing paper using your registration technique. Put the block in its correct place **ink side up** with the paper lowered in the correct place over the top. Burnish as normal or pass through a press.

19. Leave the first colour to dry and wipe clean the ink from the first block.

20. When dry, you can prepare for printing the second colour. Ink up the second block using the second colour ink.

21. Place your block in the correct place **ink side up** using your registration technique and the printing paper over the top, burnishing on the back to take the print or passing through a press.

22. Re-ink the block and continue to print over the top of all your prints. When finished, leave the prints to dry and clean the ink from the second block.

23. You are then ready to print the final colour from the key-block. Ink up the block using the black ink and place the block in place ink side up using your registration technique.

24. Lower the printing paper over the top and burnish as normal to add the final colour to your print. Lift up the paper and your three colour print is complete.

25. Re-ink the key-block and finish printing the third colour onto all your prints.

SEE IMAGES ON NEXT PAGE:
PICTURES OF THE THREE BLOCKS BEING PRINTED, ONE ON TOP OF THE OTHER. FIRSTLY THE LIGHT BLUE, THEN DARK BLUE AND FINALLY BLACK ON TOP (THE KEY-BLOCK).

26. When you are finished, leave all the prints to dry and clean up your working area.

27. This small lino print used three colours - light blue, blue and black, printed in that order. Notice how there is a good amount of each colour in the final print as well as white highlights showing through.

28. The plates can be kept for use again at another time and also tried in different colours.

THE FINAL 3-COLOUR LINOCUT, CREATED USING THE KEY-BLOCK SYSTEM THIS IMAGE SHOWS ALL THREE COLOURS - LIGHT BLUE, DARK BLUE AND FINALLY THE KEY-BLOCK IN BLACK (PRINTED LAST).

▶ **Susan's Tip...**

"A good way to check how your print will look is to proof each colour onto a sheet of acetate or tracing paper and leave to dry. When you place the sheets over each other you will have an idea how the three colours will work with each other."

'DANCER' (LINOCUT), SUSAN YEATES, 2011 - 11.5CM X 20.5CM
THE BLACK KEY-BLOCK WAS CUT FIRST AND THE PINK BACKGROUND BLOCK CUT SECOND. DURING PRINTING, THE PINK WAS PRINTED FIRST AND THE BLACK ON THE TOP USING A SIMPLE REGISTRATION METHOD.

▶ Multiple Plate Printing - Without Key-Block

It is not essential to use the key-block system to create multiple-colour prints. Try instead preparing two, three or even four separate blocks using tracing paper and carbon paper from your original design or even freely drawing and cutting the blocks.

For example, prepare a colour drawing of your print before starting. In this drawing clearly mark out using colour inks or paints where each of your colours will be. Then for each colour, trace around the edges of the colour using a pencil onto tracing paper so that you have a separate tracing for each colour. When you place these tracings over each other they should line up and you can begin to imagine how your final print will look. You can then transfer the tracing for each colour using carbon paper onto the separate blocks for your print. There should be a separate block for each colour.

Cut each block as usual and then proof each block separately before finally trying a proof using all colours. Always try to print with the lightest colour first unless you are looking to achieve a certain result.

'The Great Spotted Woodpecker' (4 block Linocut), Max Angus 20.5cm x 24.5cm

'Suffolk II' (3 block Linocut), Colin Moore - 67cm x 51cm

'The Gardener' (2 block Linocut), Richenda Court, 2008 - 60cm x 46cm

Inking Techniques and Tips

In addition to rolling one flat colour on the surface of your lino, you can also experiment with the number of colours applied and the way that you apply them. In some instances this helps to create a sense of depth within a print or even an entirely different atmosphere. Also, refer back to the section on ink in **Chapter 1** for the different qualities that can be produced from the inks themselves. e.g. gloss-finish or transparent inks.

▶ Double-Printing

As suggested by the title, you simply print the block twice (with no alterations) on one piece of paper so that both colours print directly on top of each other. The adjustment will be with the colour of inks that you use for each layer. This technique can create a richness of colour not easily created by printing in one colour only. Often when you print the second colour it may be misaligned slightly from the first giving an additional quality almost like a 3D effect. Experiment with different colours printed over the top of each other (i.e. dark over light and vice verce) and see the results. Translucent inks work well for this.

▶ Jigsaw Blocks

One way of creating separate areas of colour is to actually cut the lino into several smaller pieces to create a 'jigsaw' of blocks. Try cutting up the block just before printing (then you know that the design will register correctly). Use a craft knife and a ruler or a pair of strong scissors to cut the lino. Ink each piece of the jigsaw separately and print at the same time.

'3 Trees' (Double Printed Linocut), Linda Gresham, 2010 - 8cm x 10cm

> ▶ **Susan's Tip…**
> "Try printing your block in one colour and then turning it around a different way to print over the top with a translucent ink to see the result."

'Lantern' (Linocut), Sue Molloy, 2007 - 17.5cm x 23cm. This linoprint was created using two blocks: one block for the black and the other for the coloured background. The colour block was cut into two 'jigsaw' pieces along the perspecitve lines and inked separately before printing.

▶ 'Rainbow' Rolling Technique

'No More Fishing VII' (4 Colour Linocut), Colin Moore - 45cm x 35cm - Notice the use of 'rainbow' rolling for the sand and the sky

▶ How to do Rainbow Rolling

This is a great technique for creating beautiful backgrounds and incorporating graduated colours into landscapes or sunsets on a print. It can give a print a little more depth and colour from just one simple block. The technique can be done with two, three or more colours.

1. Choose two colours that you want to use and with a palette knife spread a small amount of each colour onto your printing surface next to each other.

2. Using a roller slightly larger than your plate, begin to roll out the two colours next to each other, making sure that you use the roller in one direction only. Slightly move the roller sideways so that the two colours begin to blend into each other.

3. When your 'rainbow' of the two inks is prepared, carefully transfer the ink onto the lino block, making sure to roll only in one direction. Build up the layers of ink on the block so that it is ready to print.

▶ Multiple Colours and Multiple Rollers

When inking a relief block it is important not to always use standard pre-mixed colours and apply this with one roller but to also experiment with blending and applying more than one ink on a particular block.

How this works in practice is to prepare several small amounts of different coloured inks onto your printing surface. Often it is a good idea to use a white and a dark colour with two or more others to create dark and light areas. Make sure you also have a selection of small rollers (smaller than your block).

Then using a roller for each colour or one roller for picking up one or two inks, gradually apply small amounts of ink onto the block – use the darker inks to create dark areas in your print and the light inks to create highlights. Blend or build up layers of ink on the block as you feel necessary. Roll in different directions and over the top of already applied colours until you feel that the inking compliments the design.

Print as normal. This technique will quickly give you the effect of a multiple-coloured print with just one block. However, bear in mind that you will need to do the same inking process for each print in the edition. This means that each print can look slightly different depending on the treatment of ink used.

▶ Separate Areas of Colour

If you have created a design where there are clearly separated areas of colour, rather than creating separate blocks for each colour, create one block and then when inking it up use smaller rollers to add the different colours to the different areas of the block. This generally only works where you have 'floating' areas of relief design clearly separated by cut out areas in the lino. You can ink up each little section in its separate colour creating the illusion of a complex multiple-block print when in fact you have just cleverly used the ink on one block.

Rolling out the two colours next to each other to create a 'rainbow'

Transferring the ink onto the lino block keeping the roller in one direction

The inked lino block   The printed linocut

▶ Paintbrush – Dabbing a Detail

If you have a print where you need just one simple dab or detail of a colour, it can be easier to do this in the inking stage rather than create a whole block just for this small area. An example of where you could use this would be if you are depicting some red berries on an image of green leaves (see image below).

Once your block is cut, ink the block in the main colour using a roller. Then using a paintbrush or cotton bud dab a little of the detail colour into the correct place where you want your highlight to be. Depending on the darkness of the first colour you may need to wipe away the first colour from the area before applying the dab of the second to allow it to show.

Then when you print, this little detail will show up in the different colour.

'Holly' (linocut), Susan Yeates, 2006 - 7cm x 7cm
This image for a Christmas card was created using one simple lino block. It was inked up in green using a roller as normal and then the red detail for the berries was created by dabbing a small amount of red ink using a paintbrush into the centre of the block.

▶ Hand-Colouring After Printing

Colour can also be added by hand after printing. Some printmakers will use paints such as watercolour, gouache or even marker pens to add a strong colour element to a black and white lino print.

Add the colour to the print once the ink has dried.

If you are using water-based paints onto a print using water-based inks, try not to smudge the initial print when you add the hand-colouring.

Above: Detail of 'Duvessa' (linocut), Susan Yeates, 2009
This print is primarily a black and white linocut created from one block of lino. However the blue colouring of the eye (detailed above) was created by hand-colouring the print using a small paintbrush and watercolour paint after printing.

Right: Detail of 'Salisbury phone box' (woodcut), Susan Yeates, 2006
In this image the bold red of the phone box was added usng a red marker pen after printing.

▶ Preventing Misalignment with Multiple Colours

When you print two colours that need to line up next to each other, unless you have absolutely perfect registration, it often happens that a white gap will appear in between the two colours. In other words your colours are misaligning.

If you carefully plan the cutting of your two colours before printing you can avoid this white gap. In essence you are allowing yourself some room for slight error in registration. There are two ways of doing this:

The first way is to extend the first colour you are printing slightly (by a millimetre or so) so that when the darker colour prints over the top it will cover this extended area. This method is good if you have a black foreground and you want another colour to show through in a gap in the black. The darker or black second colour will block out the extra piece of first colour. The second way is to extend the second colour that prints over the top.

Both methods are similar and both work on the principle that you allow the edges of the two colours to print over each other therefore preventing any small white gaps in between.

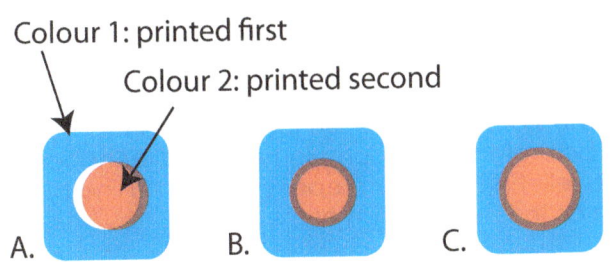

DIAGRAM ABOVE - METHODS FOR PREVENTING THE COLOURS MIS-REGISTERING.
A. COLOUR 2 HASN'T LINED UP PROPERLY LEAVING A WHITE GAP
B. COLOUR 1 HAS BEEN EXTENDED SLIGHTLY (NOTE THE OVERLAP OF THE COLOURS)
C. THE RED DOT OF COLOUR 2 HAS BEEN MADE BIGGER (I.E. EVEN IF COLOUR 2 WASN'T LINED UP NO WHITE GAP WOULD SHOW AS THERE IS A SMALL MARGIN FOR ERROR)

▶ Missed a bit?

Very often when printing there will be a small detail that doesn't print properly. This may be where you have not inked well enough, where you have not burnished properly or where a small speck of dust or lino has got into the ink creating a small circle of white.

USING A COTTON BUD WITH A SMALL AMOUNT OF PRINTING INK ON IT TO FILL IN A SMALL IMPERFECTION IN THE FINAL PRINT

If it is a small enough area you can recover the print by filling in the small area immediately after printing.

When the print is revealed after printing and you see that you have a small error, take either a cotton bud (recommended) or very small paintbrush and dab a little of the printing ink into the little white gap to cover the mistake.

By doing this when the print is still wet you can blend the ink into the printed area. Always go very slowly and gradually when dabbing on your ink and use a very small amount. This tip can be a life-saver when printing large flat areas of colour!

Experimental Linocut

In addition to creating fairly complex multi-layered prints, relief printmaking should be a creative and experimental process.

'FLOWERS 3' (MIXED MEDIA), SALLY TRASK, 2006 - 62CM x 62CM
ALL THE FLOWERS IN THIS PICTURE WERE PRINTED INDIVIDUALLY WITH DIFFERENT LINO BLOCKS

We will look at using materials and methods that are more unusual and move away from straight-forward cutting and printing. This will allow you to create very different effects and imagery.

We will look at monoprint, the use of stencils and finally alternative materials for the block. The step-by-step guides that we have included here are merely suggestions for things to try. The possibilities of experimental printmaking are endless and each printmaker has his/her own distinct style and way of working. Try to find your own style throughout the work that you do and most importantly – experiment!

▶ Incorporating Monoprint

Monoprint is a great method for combining with a lino block and another way of creating a multi-coloured, layered print from just one simple block. Monoprint is a fairly simple technique that involves rolling out or drawing with ink onto a printing surface and then laying a sheet on paper over the top to take a print. The image created is a one-off (mono) print.

A monoprint can either be printed as a first colour, a background or some of the monoprint techniques can be applied to the lino block when inking up. The painterly and spontaneous method of monoprint, however it is incorporated into your print, provides endless possibilities for experimentation.

▶ Tools and Materials

- Glass slab / other flat printing surface to work on
- Plate (glass, perspex or metal that is the size you want your print to be)
- Linoleum block
- Printing ink
- Palette knife
- Roller
- Printing paper (smooth surface)
- Roller / baren / wooden spoon for printing or press
- Tools/materials for making marks in the ink

▶ Step-by-Step Guide

In this demonstration we will look at using monoprint as a background to complement and enhance a simple relief print. Firstly prepare and cut a lino block to use as the main design of the print.

1. Plan which colours you will use for each element of the print. i.e the linoblock and the monoprint.

2. Then prepare several sheets of printing paper all exactly the same size, and prepare your registration method.

3. When your lino block, paper and ink are all prepared you can begin to start the monoprint element of your print. Use a piece of glass the same size as your lino block or a size that will complement your design. N.B If you are using a press to print do not use glass as it will smash in the printing process – instead use a sheet of metal or plastic.

4. Ink up the glass plate using a roller and then use a palette knife, paintbrush or any other tool to draw into the ink, scraping areas away and creating textures and shapes. Create the background that will complement your lino block.

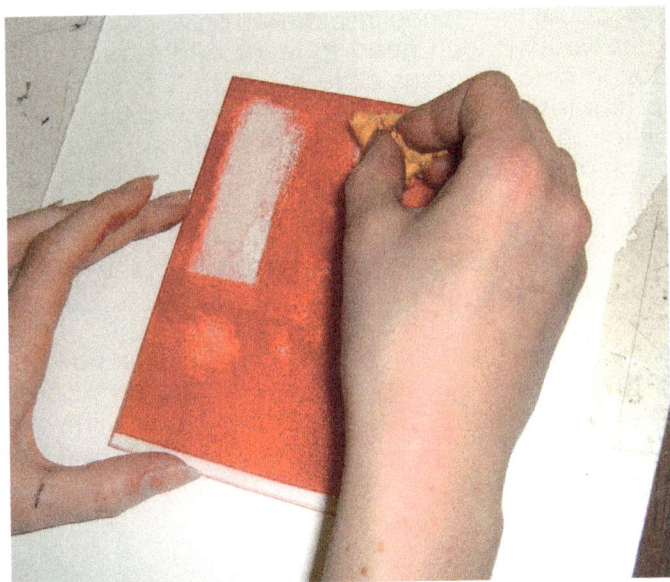

CREATING THE MONOPRINT LAYER: WIPING AREAS OF THE INK OFF THE GLASS PLATE USING A SMALL PIECE OF CLOTH. THE LINO BLOCK WAS USED AS A GUIDE.

APPLYING RED INK TO A SMALL GLASS PLATE THE SAME SIZE AS THE LINO BLOCK. IN THIS IMAGE THE LINO BLOCK IS SAT UNDERNEATH THE GLASS SHEET.

5. When your drawing in the ink is ready on the glass plate, place it **ink side up** in the centre of the backing sheet you have prepared for registration. Place the first sheet of printing paper over the top and rub on the back to take the print. Leave the monoprint background to dry in a warm flat place. If you are using a press use a sheet of perspex, plastic or metal for the monoprint instead.

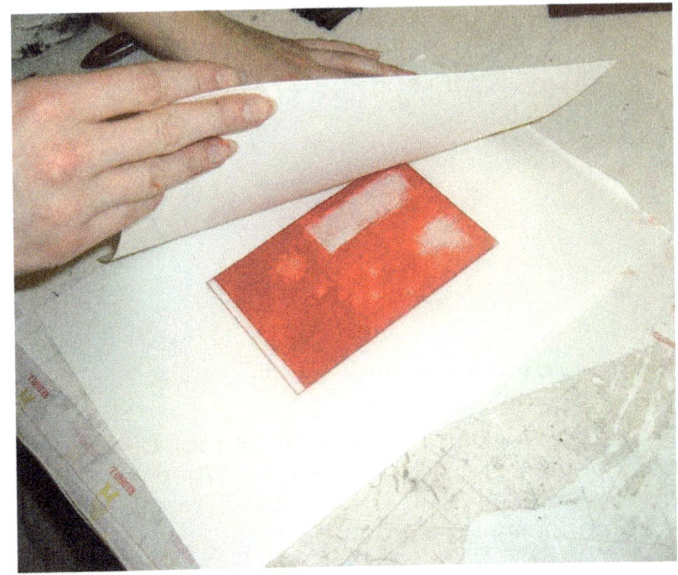

LOWER THE PRINTING PAPER DOWN ONTO THE MONOPRINT TO TAKE THE PRINT – DONE BY HAND-BURNISHING IN THIS INSTANCE.

Learning Linocut | p79

6. Because the monoprint plate will only produce one print, you will then need to re-ink and re-draw the design onto the glass plate to create backgrounds for the rest of your edition. These backgrounds can either be the same or completely different to make each of your prints unique.

7. When all the monoprint backgrounds are printed, wipe clean the glass and prepare the lino block ready for printing.

8. Ink up the lino using a roller and place **ink side up** in the centre of the backing sheet you have been using for registration. Lay the printing paper with your monoprint background on it over the top to line up the second colour.

Lowering the inked block down onto the monoprint background ('cheats' registration). This is then carefully turned over to hand-burnish

INKING UP THE LINO BLOCK IN BLACK INK

9. Using a wooden spoon or similar tool, burnish the back of the paper to take the print. When you lift the paper, the relief print will be printed over the top of your monoprint background.

Alternatively you can use a press to print both colours.

LIFTING THE FINAL PRINT UP FROM THE LINO BLOCK

10. Re-ink the block again and finish printing the second colour to finish your edition.

THE FINAL PRINT (FRAMED)
THE BLACK SECOND COLOUR HAS PRINTED OVER THE TOP OF THE RED MONOPRINT BACKGROUND.

▶ Monoprint on the Lino Block

Try using the monoprint technique on the lino block instead of separately. Either roll the ink on the block using a roller and wipe some off in areas (negative method) or apply it using a paintbrush or sponge (positive method).

Applying the ink in these different ways instead of using a roller can enhance and improve a simple linocut by clever use of colour and texture.

▶ Incorporating Stencils

Paper or acetate stencils can also be incorporated into relief printing. The two ways that stencils can be used are:

1. The stencil can be used to **block out an area** of a print so that only a part of the block prints.

2. A stencil shape can be **cut and inked separately** and then placed on top of a relief block to add a touch of a different colour.

▶ Tools and Materials

- Glass slab / other flat printing surface to work on
- Linoleum block
- Printing ink
- Palette knife
- Roller
- Printing paper (smooth surface)
- Roller / baren / wooden spoon for printing or press
- Tools/materials for making marks in the ink
- Paper or thin acetate for the stencil
- Craft knife / scalpel
- Cutting mat

▶ Step-by-Step Guide

1. Prepare and cut a simple lino block.

2. Prepare several sheets of printing paper and mark out your registration.

3. Print the lino block in a light colour. Print several copies and leave to dry. Wipe clean the block once you have finished printing so that it is clean.

4. Then using the lino block as a guide place a sheet of paper or thin acetate over the block and mark the areas you wish to cut out for your stencil using a permanent marker pen.

5. Using a craft knife and cutting mat, carefully cut out the stencil from the paper or acetate sheet.

6. When the stencil is prepared, ink up the block as usual using a second darker colour. Place this in the marked area of your backing paper.

7. Then carefully lay the stencil over the top in the correct place.

8. Lower the printing paper (with the first colour on it) over the top and burnish from the back to take the print.

This process can then be repeated, re-using the stencil again, to complete your edition of prints. This is a quick way to produce a simple two-colour print with just one set of cuts to the block.

▶ Demonstration Using Stencils to Block Out Areas of the Print

This demonstration uses 2 separate cut lino blocks in combination with stencils to produce a larger print.

THE SECOND LINO BLOCK INKED UP IN YELLOW BUT WITH AN ACETATE STENCIL PLACED OVER THE CENTRE PART TO BLOCK THIS PRINTING

THE PRINT AFTER PRINTING THE FIRST COLOUR (RED) AND SECOND COLOURS (YELLOW)

THE PRINT AFTER A THIRD COLOUR (GREEN) IS PRINTED

NOTE THAT A SIMPLE PENCIL LINE HAS BEEN USED TO LINE UP THE BLOCKS NEXT TO EACH OTHER ON THE PAPER. THIS IN COMBINATION WITH THE CHEATS' REGISTRATION HAS ALLOWED ALL THE COLOURS IN THE PRINT TO REGISTER CORRECTLY.

THE FIRST COLOUR (RED) INKED ONTO ONE OF THE BLOCKS WITH AN ACETATE STENCIL BLOCKING CERTAIN AREAS OF THE PLATE. ONLY THE END THIRD OF THE BLOCK WILL PRINT.

THIS IMAGE SHOWS SOME BLACK INK BEING TRANSFERRED TO ONE OF THE BLOCKS FROM THE OTHER (NOT SHOWN). THE OTHER BLOCK WAS INKED UP IN BLACK AND THE ACETATE PLACED OVER THE TOP. THE INK WAS THEN TRANSFERRED TO THE END OF THE BLOCK SHOWN BEFORE BEING PRINTED ONTO THE FINAL PRINTING PAPER.

THE FINISHED PRINT USING STENCILS

This print demonstrates the possibilities of using stencils in combination with lino blocks. Sections of the block were either completely masked out using acetate stencils or a different coloured ink was transferred from one block to another before printing onto the final print. Try both this and the other method of using stencils.

▶ White Ink on Black Paper

Rather than using black (or coloured) ink onto a white paper, it can be very effective to work in reverse i.e. printing with a white-based ink onto black paper. The entire process of cutting and printing is the same, the only difference is that you chose white printing ink (or add a small amount of another colour for variation) rather than black for printing.

A SMALL LINOCUT PRINT USING WHITE INK PRINTED ONTO BLACK PAPER

An alternative is to print a black or dark coloured background first using black or dark ink on an uncut linoblock, allow this to dry and then print in white your cut block over the top.

'THE PETWORTH OWL' (LINOPRINT AND MONOPRINT), RUTH BARRETT-DANES, 2010 - 20CM x 20CM

NOTE FROM THE ARTIST: "THIS IMAGE WAS A COMBINATION OF MONOPRINT AND A LINOCUT USING THE JAPANESE VINYL MATERIAL AVAILABLE FROM INTAGLIO PRINTMAKER. THIS MATERIAL HAS TWO USABLE SIDES AND MEANT THAT ONE SIDE COULD BE USED FOR THE MONOPRINT AND THEN THE LINOCUT SIDE PRINTED ENSURING A PERFECT SIZE FIT AND REGISTRATION."

▶ Chine Collè

Chine Collé is a technique that allows printmakers to add areas of thin (often coloured) paper to a print, very similar to a collage. These thin pieces of paper are placed between the ink and the printing paper before printing so that they stick to the paper but the ink is printed on top.

After preparing a lino block, place it ink-side up onto the press bed. Thin 'collage' paper with glue or a paste solution applied to one side is then placed on top of the inked block, glue side up. Finally the printing paper is placed on top of the lino block so that you have a sandwich where the printing paper is at the top, the lino at the bottom and the collage paper is sandwiched in between. This is then passed through the press. The pressure of the press will take the print from the lino but also stick the thin area of collage paper to the printing paper behind the ink.

Chine Collé will allow you to add small pieces of tissue, found papers or newspaper to complement your design or you may even want a large coloured background to your print.

'The Enchantment of the Moon - Turquoise' (Linocut with chine colle), Liz Toole, 2011 - 75cm x 55cm. In this print chine colle was used to create the white colour behind the birds and the moon. This is printed onto turquoise paper.

▶ Etching into Lino

The process of etching can also be used with lino as an alternative method for working into the block. This process should be treated with care and with proper safety precautions (seek advice or supervision at a professional pintmaking studio where possible) due to the strength and corrosive nature of the chemicals used.

The lino block is degreased and using wax or stop-out varnish, areas of the relief block are protected i.e. the areas that you wish to remain in relief are covered in wax. The sides and back of the lino bock are also protected with either parcel tape, PVA glue or the stop-out varnish.

A strong etching solution (such as caustic soda) is then applied to the block. Where the lino is exposed it will 'bite' into the block creating 'cuts' and leaving the protected areas in relief. Leave this to etch into the lino for the appropriate time and then thoroughly wash the lino block.

This method can often create lino blocks that either have a more painterly feel to them or a very textured finish depending on the length of time that the block is left in the etching solution. Alternatively, the etching solution can be painted directly on to the block without using wax to block out areas first.

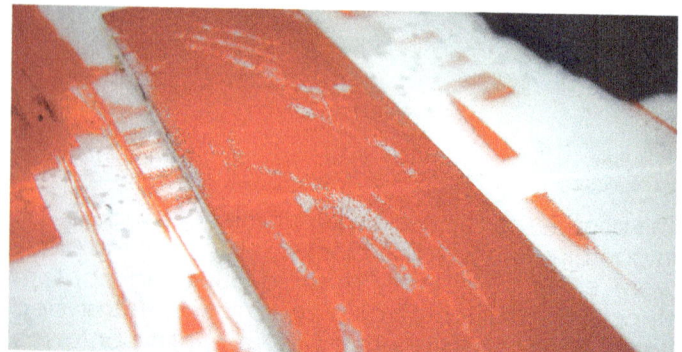

An etched lino block inked up - note the texture created by the etching process

▶ Other Materials for the Block

In addition to using linoleum (lino) for your relief block, other materials have some interesting and challenging qualities for your prints. Think creatively when choosing another material – look around you to see what sorts of materials are available that you could carve into with your cutting tools.

Whatever material you choose to use, treat it in exactly the same way as a lino block – the only difference may be your cutting technique and inking may take a little practice if the material is textured, soft or generally different in appearance to lino.

Try some of the following materials:

▶ Woodcut

Wood is fairly inexpensive, varied and widely available for relief printing. The main difference between lino and wood is that wood has a grain running through it adding a particular character to each print. Because of this you will find that it will be easier to cut in one direction, along the grain, rather than across it. Therefore it is often helpful to design your images to work with or along the grain.

Before cutting into a wood block, prepare the block by sanding the surface and edges to make it smooth. To enhance the character of the grain use some wire wool. Apply a thin coat of ink or paint to the top before cutting and allow to dry. Then when you cut into the wood you can see your cuts more clearly.

▶ Types of Wood

Plywood - Plywood panels are composed of thin layers of wood glued together at right angles to create a thicker, flatter sheet. Plywood is available in many different thicknesses and the thicker the plywood the more expensive and flat the wood. Japanese plywood is popular as it is fairly soft to cut and inexpensive to buy.

Solid Plank of Wood - It is the side grain of the wood that is used for woodcut printing i.e. the wood is cut down its length and the grain of the wood will run along the print. It is wood engraving that uses the end grain of a piece of wood.

Softwoods including pine, spruce, cedar and fir are less expensive than hardwoods and generally thought to be easier to carve into. Materials like pine often have a very strong grain and knots, which can be incorporated into your design. Even old pine furniture can be used for cutting into as it has been seasoned for a long period making it unlikely to warp and bend.

Hardwoods including basswood, maple and cherry are harder woods and will enable fine detail to be carved into them. They are slightly more expensive and will mean your tools need sharpening (or throwing away) more regularly.

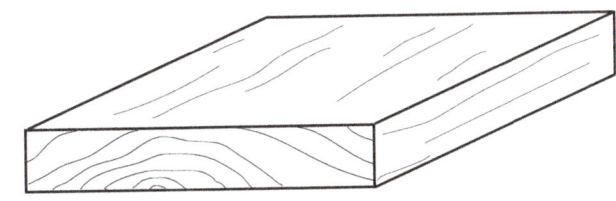

Solid plank of wood

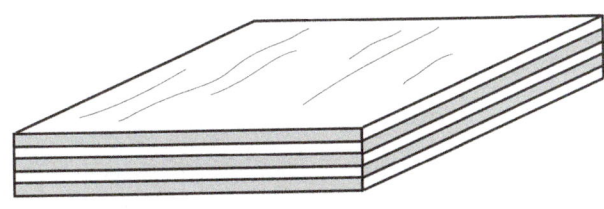

Plywood

▶ Susan's Suggestions...

"Why not try some of these materials instead of lino to see what interesting results you can get?"

Cardboard - Both corrugated cardboard and thick flat card that will hold cuts, can be very interesting materials to work with. Use a knife to cut into the board to create marks and be aware that water-based ink may cause the card to warp. A coat of PVA glue on the card may prevent too much ink soaking into it.

Polystyrene - Polystyrene is often found as packaging and is fairly soft to cut into. It is usually made up of smaller pieces that are pressed together and these shapes will print an interesting texture. Just be careful when burnishing, because if you press too hard the polystyrene may damage.

Chipboard - Chipboard is easily found in DIY stores and made from chips of wood glued together into a flat board. Chipboard can be very hard to cut and will not allow you to cut a detailed image. However if you are looking for a large block that you can use, or for an interesting texture, this can be worth a try.

MDF (Medium Density Fibreboard) - Similar to chipboard but slightly smoother, MDF is readily available in large sheets from DIY stores. Again this will be hard to cut and produce cuts with blurred edges but can be an interesting block to try out.

Erasers (rubbers) - Found in most stationary shops, these can be great fun to use as small relief blocks. Soft to cut they can be great for greeting cards, adding detail to a larger plate or just for miniature prints.

Vinyl / Styrofoam - Vinyl and styrofoam are materials supplied by printmaking and art suppliers that are often used in schools as an alternative to lino. They are softer and easier to cut than lino or wood and produce a good quality print.

Plastic - Some plastics will be soft enough to cut into using a craft knife or your cutting tools. Plastic can be an interesting surface to use, with varying effects.

Found objects - Any object with a soft enough or wooden surface can be carved into and printed from. You may need to print by stamping the object down or if the object is unusually shaped almost wrap the paper around before burnishing.

Fruits and Vegetables - Why not try potato printing? Fruits and vegetables can prove to be very interesting materials to work from. Just make sure the surface of your vegetable is as dry as possible before applying the ink to give you a better coverage.

Plaster of Paris - Create a flat block to work from (pour the mixed plaster into a flat mould such as a tray) and sandpaper the surface to make it smooth to work into. You will be carving instead of cutting the plaster so work slowly and carefully.

Plasticine - Plasticine is a soft modelling paste/clay that is used by children and for sculpting. Work the plasticine until soft and pliable, then smooth or roll out into a flat surface to work from. The plasticine can then be cut or pressed into to create marks. The disadvantage of plasticine is that it remains soft so when printing you may need to be fairly careful.

'Fimo' modelling clay - Fimo is another type of modelling clay that is often used for creating finer work such as jewellery or small detailed models. After modelling, the clay is put in the oven to dry out and create a completely solid piece. This will then give you the solid relief block to print from. It has a smooth paste like texture and holds a shape very well.

Chapter 4: The Finished Linocut

In this chapter we will look at what happens after the creative process of producing your linocuts. To start with we will explain how to finish off an edition of prints and then discuss storing and presenting your work in various ways. Finally, we will introduce selling and pricing prints and mention some other techniques that you may also like to explore now that you have the printmaking bug!

'River by Moonlight' (Linocut), David Browning, 2007 - 18cm x 19.5cm

'Deal' (3 Block Linocut), Colin Moore - 45cm x 65cm

Learning Linocut | p87

Editioning

With linocut you will produce a series of more than one identical or near-identical prints. This is called an edition. An edition can be as few as 3 to 4 or as many as several hundred. On average most printmakers produce an edition of between 10 and 50.

Most printmakers will experiment in the studio, producing many proofs or trials of a design until they are 100% happy with it. This may take several days or weeks to achieve. Once this is done then they will return to their studio space with a decision on the paper to be used, the number in the edition to produce and the whole edition will then be printed and complete. It is a good idea to work in the same manner for linocut, taking the time to try out different colours, papers, inking techniques and then return to complete printing the whole edition.

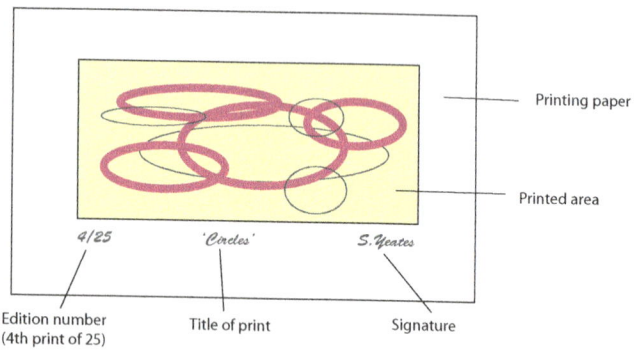

DIAGRAM OF AN 'EDITIONED' PRINT

Traditionally, editions of prints are numbered and signed by the artist, usually in pencil. The purpose of editioning a series of prints is to let an audience know how many prints in the edition were printed. It also confirms that no more will be printed and often blocks are marked or destroyed after the edition is complete. Therefore, once your whole edition of linocuts is printed, you title and sign your prints in this way to finish them off.

If you have any proofs or copies that you have produced of a particular print that are spare and separate to the edition, write A/P (which stands for artist's proof) where the edition number would normally be. Sometimes a number of artists proofs are produced for keeping yourself or handing to friends or family. Once the full edition has been produced it is standard to destroy the original lino blocks by either cutting a hole or damaging mark into them so that the edition cannot be continued i.e. the blocks are no longer usable.

Presenting and Storing Work

Presenting your prints in a professional manner is the final stage in a print's creation and the way a print is presented can have a major influence on its appreciation by an audience.

A badly presented print with inky finger marks, wonky mounting or bad framing can spoil the appearance of a perfectly good print. Likewise, a neat, well-presented, professionally framed print where the frame enhances and complements the print design, will look outstanding and 'wow' an audience. You must therefore take care when printing, storing and finally framing a print that it is done in both a professional and organised way.

'TWILIGHT' (LINOCUT), SUSAN YEATES, 2008 - 4.5CM x 7CM

▶ Keeping Clean and Tidy

It is essential when printmaking that you experiment a lot and fully explore the technique you are using. The creative process must be allowed room to flow correctly and this sometimes means making a mess! However, it is also very important to end up with prints that are clean and tidy so that they are presentable for selling or exhibiting.

In **Chapter 1** we demonstrated a good way to layout your desk space for printing. Make sure that you use this method or a similar set-up to keep clean paper away from wet ink and water and prevent accidents with sharp tools and solvents. Don't forget that some materials can also be expensive and you do not want to waste or ruin good quality materials through bad organisation.

By employing one of the registration techniques from **Chapter 2** this will ensure that your prints are firstly registered correctly nearly every time but also ensure that the edges of the print are clean and free from ink marks, thereby saving paper. The area around your linocut print to the edges of the paper should always be clean and free from finger marks, ink marks, pencil marks or general dirt. A good way to work is to always print onto paper a good deal larger than your print, so that if you pick up the edges of the paper with inky fingers, you can always trim the paper and crop off any finger marks that would spoil the final presentation.

▶ Tips for keeping clean and tidy

- Always wipe up any unused ink from the area you are working and clean up thoroughly after printing.
- Never store wet prints on top of each other as they can become stuck together and damaged.
- Try to work on paper larger than you need so that any unwanted ink marks from edges can be trimmed.
- Always trim paper with a **sharp knife** to prevent tearing.
- If you are a messy worker use small pieces of scrap paper between the printing paper and your fingers to stop marks or wear gloves when printing which you can then remove to handle the clean paper.
- Keep all finished prints in a safe, clean and dry place away from your printing ink and any water.
- Rub out any pencil marks that you used for registration from your final print.

CLEANING UP YOUR INK AFTER PRINTING (FOR OIL-BASED INKS)
1. SCRAPE AWAY ANY SPARE INK WITH A PALETTE KNIFE AND THROW AWAY.
2. WHILST WEARING LATEX OR PLASTIC GLOVES, USE A GENEROUS AMOUNT OF VEGETABLE OIL AND POUR ONTO THE PRINTING SURFACE. USE A SCRAP CLOTH OR DIRTY RAG TO LOOSEN THE INK AND THEN WIPE IT AWAY FROM THE PRINTING SURFACE.
3. ONCE THIS IS DONE USE A SMALL AMOUNT OF WHITE SPIRIT AND A CLEAN CLOTH TO CLEAN AWAY ANY RESIDUE INK TO LEAVE A SPOTLESS SURFACE FOR PRINTING NEXT TIME.
4. USE OIL AND WHITE SPIRIT TO CLEAN YOUR ROLLERS, PALETTE KNIVES AND LINO BLOCKS.
5. FOR WATER-BASED INKS INSTEAD USE WATER AND A CLOTH TO WIPE AWAY ANY INK.

▶ Susan's Tip…

"If you do end up with inky marks that you are unable to trim, use a small piece of fine sandpaper and rub the printing paper gently to take away the mark. It may take a little practice and patience so try on some test paper first before correcting a final print. If the print still has bad marks that you cannot remove, clever framing and mounting may hide the mistake."

▶ Storing Prints

We discussed in **Chapter 1** about storing paper, inks and other materials in a safe and careful way. This is even more important with the finished prints that you have produced. Prints need to be treated with great care and attention if you want them to stay in good condition.

Bear in mind the following points:

- Keep all prints out of direct sunlight to prevent fading and UV damage to the paper.
- Keep them in a dry, cool place free from any water, condensation, steam or damp.
- If you are storing prints together, make sure that they have sheets of acid-free tissue in between them.
- Make sure all prints are fully dry before you store them.
- Use a plan chest, portfolio or simple drawer system for storing finished work flat.
- If you are working very large, you may need to roll prints up. If so, make sure that you use acid-free tissue paper in between the print as well.
- Keep all finished prints away from ink, chemicals or anything that could spill onto them and damage the prints.
- Do not handle finished prints with oily or sticky fingers as this will damage the paper.

'SO THICK WITH CORN THEY LAUGH AND SING' (LINOCUT), MAX ANGUS - 60 x 30CM

▶ Framing Prints

Lino prints are a 2D art form and to present them well often requires framing. This is especially true if you are looking to display work in an exhibition or on the walls of your own home. A good frame will show off a print, complement its design and also protect it from damage. When choosing a frame for a print spend a good amount of time selecting the thickness, colour and type of frame that will best suit the work.

Professional framing companies will be able to offer you good advice as to the colour of frame that will enhance the colours in the image and protect the work properly. They nearly always have small corner samples of frames that you can place next to the print to see what works well with the design.

TRYING OUT A MOUNT AND FRAME COMBINATION ON A PRINT IN A FRAMING STUDIO. THE PRINT HERE WORKS WELL WITH A SIMPLE BLACK FRAME AND A DOUBLE MOUNT THAT COMPLEMENTS AND PICKS OUT THE BLACK HORIZONTAL AND VERTICAL LINES OF THE IMAGE.

Frames come in unstained wood, stained wood, aluminium and plastic with all types of mouldings and finishings, so it is very much dependent on the type of work you produce as to the particular frame that will complement and enhance the print the best.

A PRINT BEING FRAMED AT OTTERS POOL STUDIO, PICTURE FRAMERS IN GUILDFORD, SURREY

Prints can also be framed in box frames that are a lot deeper than normal frames and will help to show off very textured work or layered work that may not fit a standard frame. Sometimes even 'float' mounting a piece of work on paper is very effective as it will allow the deckled edges of a high quality piece of hand-made paper to show.

There are also a variety of glass types available to place in front of the print - some of which are anti-reflective or even UV protective.

Prints are very often framed in combination with a mount. A mount is a piece of mount board cut into a frame shape, that is placed in front of the print to both frame it and prevent the print from touching the glass. This is usually in line with the print with just a little extra space at the bottom of the print to allow the signature and title to show. Mounts come in different colours to complement the design of your print and the frame. More than one mount can be used in combination to surround a print, (double mounting or triple mounting) to add a little strip or strips of colour near the edge of the print.

Paper can swell with time so usually a print will be taped at the top corners behind the mount to keep it in place but allow for it to breathe. Always choose acid-free mount board to use with your prints.

Your choice of frame and mount will very much depend on the final print you produce. It is also a question of personal preference and taste and dependent on the final place that the print is to be hung. If you are framing some work for an exhibition for example, always check with the curator or exhibition organiser what their framing and presentation requirements are.

A frame is the finishing touch that will absolutely complete a print and it is well worth spending the time picking the best one for your work, whether this is shop bought or bespoke from a picture framers.

SAMPLES OF FRAMES THAT ARE AVAILABLE FOR FINISHING YOUR PRINTS

▶ Other Ways to Finish and Present Prints

In addition to framing, you can also present and finish your prints in other ways including:

▶ Cellophane Wrapping

When presenting your prints for sale but unframed, a good idea is to wrap them in some cellophane for protection. Trim your final print at the edges to make them neat, although wherever possible, avoid cutting off the 'deckled' edges of hand-made papers. Back this with a piece of strong grey card or mount board to prevent it from bending and then wrap it with cellophane securing the edges at the back with some masking tape or sellotape. A mount can be placed in front of the print before wrapping to 'frame' it.

It is a good idea to place a label on the back listing the details of the print including the price, type of print (e.g. linocut), your name, date and the title of the work. Cellophane can be obtained in rolls from your local art shop or craft shop. Alternatively use the types of cello bags used to wrap greetings cards if your print is small enough.

This can often be a much cheaper way to present your prints than framing and will keep them in good condition until the print is bought, but still looking attractive.

▶ Greetings Cards

There are two main approaches you can have to producing greetings cards from your linocut prints:

1. Design small blocks especially for use on cards - By designing an image specifically for use on greetings cards you can keep reproducing the image until you have enough of a particular design. You can either buy greetings cards ready-cut or buy larger sheets of card and cut to size. Look to produce cards of standard sizes such as A6 as you will be able to find envelopes and cello bags that are the correct size.

Will you have a border of white around the design and the image in the middle? Or will the pattern cover the whole card?

EXAMLES OF GREETINGS CARDS PRODUCED USING SMALL LINO BLOCKS AT A ONE-DAY PRINTMAKING WORKSHOP. STUDENTS PRINTED DIRECTLY ONTO THE CARDS AND ALSO ONTO SEPARATE PIECES OF PAPER READY TO BE MOUNTED ON CARDS WITH PRE-CUT WINDOWS.

2. Cut up larger or unwanted prints and turn these into cards - As well as designing especially for cards, you can also cut up unwanted prints, scraps and larger prints. These can then be trimmed to size and either glued to the middle of a blank card with a good border around or the whole larger print can be folded in two, to create the card. You can easily make a selection of cards from wasted paper and scraps that you may have decided to throw away. It may be a print that you started but only liked a small section of it, so use this to stick onto a card. It may also be a spare copy of a large patterned print where you may have smudged an area so that you can't display it as a print on its own.

Creating greetings cards is a great way to send people a piece of original art and for you to show your work to many people. Greetings cards can also be sold to people interested in your work who may not be able to afford or want a larger piece of work.

▶ Wrapping Paper, Gift Bags and Bookmarks

Prints or printing blocks can be used very effectively to create unique wrapping paper and with a little careful folding, gift bags as well. Simply print a small lino block several times in a repeat onto a good quality paper or tissue to create a full sheet of wrapping paper (see **Chapter 2** for details of repeat patterns). You can also create good bookmarks from small off-cuts of larger prints or specially designed small prints.

USING A SMALL RELIEF BLOCK TO CREATE A LARGE SHEET OF WRAPPING PAPER IN A PRINTMAKING WORKSHOP

▶ Artist's Books

Prints can also be made or incorporated into artist's books. These are handmade, usually hand-bound books containing a series of prints, images or relevant text. There are a multitude of ways of bookbinding including creating a zig-zag book, sewing a proper spine and even pop-ups. You can use the prints to illustrate a particular story or simply another creative way to display your prints.

▶ Printing onto Fabric

Once you start to really develop your printmaking, you may decide that you wish to start printing onto fabric. You will need to speak to a local supplier about the types of fabric that you can print onto and the types of inks and pigments that you will need to use. However, the basic principles are the same as printing onto paper and your designs for paper can be translated onto fabric for use within the home or for example on simple handbags or t-shirts.

▶ General Presentation Advice

It greatly depends on what and where you are displaying your work as to how you present it as a whole. As a general guide, when displaying framed work, make sure that your work is easy to see e.g. not too high or too low (the average eye-level for hanging a work is 150cm from the floor) so make sure that the viewer does not have to bend or strain too much to see the work.

If you have unframed prints or even greetings cards to display, use a portfolio, simple clean box, basket or stand to hold the prints and cards allowing the viewer to flick through them easily. Don't forget to make sure that works are protected using clear plastic so that they don't gather sticky finger marks from people picking them up to look closer. Always display a few works clearly for the viewer to see even if the rest are in boxes or portfolios.

As a general rule, use simple black or white backgrounds behind whatever work you display. This will encourage the colours of the prints to stand out and people to focus on the work itself rather than become distracted by the background behind.

Never crowd too many works together at once, as the viewer's eye will not know what image to look at first.

If you are arranging an exhibition or display yourself, take great care when preparing the display and try it out first to see which arrangement works the best. Always take time out to step back and see what stands out and whether the arrangement is pleasing to the eye. Choose a logical arrangement that is clear and crisp allowing the merits of the prints to be properly enhanced.

FRAMED LINOCUT PRINTS ON DISPLAY IN A CAFE

Also make sure that prints are hung straight (use a spirit level to check if you are unsure), framed where possible to enhance the prints or in the cases of other works show them off in the best possible way. E.g. with t-shirts maybe use a mannequin to display an example t-shirt on or wear one yourself. With greetings cards, investigate buying a proper stand if you have many to display.

If appropriate, you will need to look at either price tags, labels or small cards with the description and/or price on – be creative with this if you can but always make it clear, neat and easy to understand.

Take pride in your work and show it off to its best advantage to allow your viewers to appreciate it as much as you do.

RIGHT: 'LADY IN BLUE' (LINOCUT), JACKIE BROWNING, 2007 - 14CM x 16.5CM DETAIL OF A SIMPLE BUT EFFECTIVE LINOCUT PRINT PRODUCED DURING A 10-WEEK LINOCUT COURSE IN 2007.

 ## Selling Your Work

Do not forget that prints are essentially a form of affordable art and selling work is a great way to firstly help begin to pay for your materials and tools, but also to gain feedback on your work and engage in a critical dialogue with your audience. As you progress, you will start to gain recognition as an artist and printmaker and steadily carve out a career or develop it into a serious hobby.

The key is to start small and begin by giving prints away as presents to friends, family and colleagues. Possibly turn your smaller prints into greetings cards for all sorts of occasions or into business cards for promoting yourself.

Seek also to apply to open exhibitions to get your framed prints displayed in local galleries and venues around the country.

Try as much as you can to gain opinion and criticism of your work. Start with friends and family or seek out other printmakers, artists and printmaking studios near you to join in a community of artists. Renting a studio space in shared studios can be a great place to work, as well as a way of engaging with other artists.

▶ Costing and Pricing Your Work

If you intend to make a profit from your artwork, you will need to calculate exactly how much each item costs to produce. To work out the cost, you must include the materials you use, your time spent making each work plus a small allowance towards other costs you incur through making the works such as electricity, your general marketing expenses and share of the wear and tear to tools and equipment.

Use the basic table below to work out how much each print you make costs. When working out the cost of your time, multiply the time you spend making the item by an estimated hourly rate. To work out the contribution to tools, take the cost of the item (e.g. the lino cutters) and divide this by the number of works you estimate that this will last for. Adding all these up will then give you an estimate of the cost of the work to make.

Paper	
Inks	
Other materials	
Time (hrs x your hourly rate)	
Contribution towards electricity etc	
Contribution towards tools etc	
Other expenses	
Total Cost	

You then need to look to roughly double this cost price to find the price to sell your work for, e.g. if your cost price turns out to be £10 you need to charge at least £20 to make a good profit.

However, you must also make sure that you do not out price yourself from the market, so that no-one buys your work thinking it too expensive. Do some research in your local area to find our how much artists around you are charging for similar works before setting your final prices for your prints and other works.

Trade prices and retail prices: Some shops and galleries you deal with may want to buy items in bulk. Therefore, instead of charging them a retail price (i.e. the price that the general public will pay), you need to work out a trade price for them to buy many products at once. For these trade orders, the retailer will want to mark up the item to the retail price to make a profit, so you need to make sure that your costs are not too high to start with. It is a good idea to make sure that you have a minimum order level when selling in bulk to make sure that you make a good level of money from each order.

Commission: You may find that some outlets will charge a commission or fee for selling your work, so bear this in mind too when setting your price. Galleries and craft venues can often charge up to 50% of a sale price, so make sure you are aware of any possible commissions when approaching galleries or exhibiting at a venue for the first time.

▶ Where to Sell Your Prints

There are some very simple and easy ways to get started selling your linocut prints. This doesn't have to cost a lot and all the methods we list here are all tried and tested ways of successfully selling original linocut prints.

- To friends and family
- At craft fairs and school fetes
- Party planning
- Your own website
- Other websites promoting prints
- Market stalls in craft venues or shopping centres
- Sale or return – shops and galleries
- Open exhibitions
- Solo or group exhibitions
- Open studios and arts trails

▶ Life after lino - Other techniques to try...

"Now that you are comfortable with linoprinting, there is no reason why you cannot try out and explore some of the other varied and interesting techniques available to you. There are four main categories that the various forms of printmaking fall into:"

1. Intaglio (etching, drypoint, solar etching, aquatint, mezzotint) - Intaglio printmaking is traditionally carried out onto a metal plate. The metal plate is marked in some way by etching or scratching and the lines that are created are the marks that print i.e. it is thought of as a positive mark making technique, although the print will still be a 'mirror image' of the original plate. These printmaking techniques are usually printed using an etching press.

Etching is the process of corroding a metal plate with acid to create marks that will hold ink before this is then printed. A hard or soft ground (acid-resistant waxy-like substance) is used to block certain areas of the plate. Where the ground is placed it resists the acid and prevents the acid from corroding the plate. Aquatint is a method of applying solid areas of tone on an etching plate.

With drypoint, a sheet of perspex or metal is directly scratched into using a needle to create a linear image and ink worked into the scratches (and burrs) before printing.

2. Relief (linocut, woodcut and wood engraving) - Relief printing in contrast to intaglio is a collection of negative techniques where the plate or block e.g. wood, is cut into to create an image. The area that is left is what prints and the cut area remains the colour of the printing paper. Several blocks can be prepared to produce multiple coloured prints. Woodcut art can be very striking and expressive, for example the dramatic effects seen in Japanese woodcut prints.

Wood engraving uses the end grain (i.e. cut across the plank) of the wood instead of using the side grain of wood (the plank). Therefore a grain is not present in the final image. The tools used are slightly different and a lot finer cuts can be made.

3. Planographic (lithography) - Lithography works on the basis that oil and water do not mix. The image and non-printing parts are on the same level but the image (drawn with an oil-based material onto either a metal plate or litho stone), is then set and printing is done either by direct contact or offsetting. Lithography requires specialist presses.

4. Stencil-Based Printing (screenprinting) - In this form of printmaking, a stencil is created onto a screen (a fine mesh of fabric stretched over a wooden or metal frame) before ink is pushed through using a squeegee. Where the stencil is placed (by hand painting, paper stencil or exposed emulsion) the ink will not pass through. This method produces images that are the same way around as the stencils. Screen printing can be performed using small screens or larger screens in combination with a vacuum/screen bed. Screen printing is also used frequently for printing onto fabric and commercial purposes such as signmaking and t-shirt printing.

5. Other techniques -
Monoprinting - Monoprinting is a simple technique that involves rolling out or drawing with ink on to a printing surface and creating a mark in varying ways. A sheet of paper is laid over the top to take a print. It can be a very painterly and free way of printing, although each print is a unique, one-off image.

Collograph - Collograph (collage prints) are simple relief prints created from printing from a collage block. The block is created by sticking various items into a cardboard base using PVA glue or similar which is then left to dry. The textured surface created is what generates the light and dark areas of the print. The plate can be inked using either the relief or intaglio method of inking.

Chapter 5: Linocut Projects and Resources

In this final chapter of **Learning Linocut** there are some interesting and helpful projects to get stuck into to develop your lincutting skills further as well as some useful resources.

The four projects, all taken and developed from live printmaking workshops, tackle a selection of skills from studying someone else's style and technique to using linocut as a form of illustration. The projects can be completed in any order or just used to generate some inspiration for your work.

The useful resources section will point you in the right direction for finding materials, printmaking studios, other books and the work of other printmakers.

▶ Susan's Final Thought

"I hope you have enjoyed 'Learning Linocut' as much as I have. Linocut is a such an interesting and varied technique that never ceases to amaze me. I wish you all the best with your printmaking. To send me images of your prints (which I would love to see) please visit: www.learninglinocut.co.uk."

'A Patchwork Print' (Linocut), Multiple Artists, 2010 (See Project 4)

Project 1: 'In the Style of...'

About this project

"This project has been set to demonstrate your understanding of interpreting style and using this to influence and inform your work."

Let's Get Started...

There is a long tradition of artists and printmakers paying homage to past masters and using their style to learn from and to influence their own work.

Visit a library, art gallery or use the internet to find an artist or period of art whose distinct style you like or wish to use as inspiration. You could choose a great 'master' (an artist who is familiar), such as Van Gogh, Turner, Munch, Matisse, Picasso or a recognisable style such as pop art or expressionism or even a printmaker who has strong ways of working that you wish to explore yourself.

Take time to gather your research, collecting images of their work and making a series of sketches and preliminary ideas using a sketchbook or idea sheets. Investigate the issues that the artist or style deals with in their work and the subject matter they choose. Carry out several studies by simply copying their work.

Look at the distinct style that they use – are there large flat areas of colour or a specific way that marks are made. Try to recreate these types of marks and shapes in your studies.

From your studies complete the following work:

- A simple linocut study
- A reduction print (minimum 2 colours)
- A key-block multiple plate print (at least 3 colours).
- A small 50-100 word artist's statement about why you chose that artist or style to study and why they inspired you. Describe the key stylistic features that you chose to then inflence your own prints.

Make sure that at least one of these prints is a direct copy of one of the artist's work and one is a print of your own subject matter but using their style.

Example Work

'AFTER VAN GOGH' (LINOCUT), DAVID BROWNING, 2007 - 12.8CM X 17CM

NOTE: THIS IMAGE WAS CREATED DURING A 10 WEEK RELIEF PRINTING COURSE. THE ARTIST CHOSE VINCENT VAN GOGH AS THEIR CHOSEN ARTIST/STYLE AND TRIED TO INTERPRET THE SENSE OF MOVEMENT THAT VAN GOGH HAS IN HIS PAINTINGS THROUGH CUTTING TECHNIQUE. THIS FINAL PRINT WAS A MULTPLE-COLOURED LINOCUT INCORPORATING THE REDUCTION TECHNIQUE.

Project 2: Old Photograph

About this project

"This project will investigate a theme or memory selected from an old photograph that captures a specific moment in time that means something to you."

Let's Get Started...

The work you complete on this project must demonstrate your understanding of relief printing in one colour (i.e. one simple block) plus how to interpret and work with a single starting point. Search through some old photographs and source a single image that you can use as your inspiration.

Find an image that shows a place or time in your life that is important to you or something that you feel strongly about. It may be an image of your children, your mother or father or grandparents. It could be a place you visited on holiday, a past pet, an old school, an old friend or even an old favourite toy. The photograph itself may have certain qualities such as torn edges, folds or faded areas. It could be black and white, colour or a picture that was discarded as not good enough for a photograph album.

From this one old photograph, begin to make a series of small pencil sketches to work out what types of marks you wish to use to recreate this image or how you wish to interpret a small part of it. Think about whether you will use negative or positive cutting to cut the design. Try making some 'mark-making' tester pieces to explore the types of cuts that you will use to create your final print. These marks should be influenced by the way you feel about the image, the age of the print or how you wish to expore or distort the final result.

You may wish to trace your image and then use the tracing paper with carbon paper underneath to transfer this on to your lino block before cutting. You may not wish to copy or recreate the image exactly but use the photograph instead as a starting point to inspire other ideas and themes. It may help to work in a sketchbook or on an idea sheet to help you to create your composition.

Once you have finished your preparatory work, use one single block of lino to create your image. You can choose to work in the same scale as your photograph i.e. A6/postcard sized or larger. If you are feeling adventurous you could explore how scale may effect your image – try recreating the image in a huge scale or even just enlarge a very small area.

Print the lino block in a single colour such as black and create an edition of at least 10 good final prints. Think of a good title for the work that captures the moment you are depicting.

Example Work

'BOOTS' (LINOCUT), SUSAN YEATES, 2008

THIS SIMPLE BLACK AND WHITE LINOPRINT WAS DEVELOPED FROM A SMALL SECTION OF AN OLD PHOTOGRAPH. THIS SMALL SECTION WAS ENLARGED TO CREATE A LARGER PRINT.

Project 3: Book Illustration

About this project

"This project uses the method of linocut to create a narrative and generate a multiple coloured book illustration."

Let's Get Started...

Relief printing (mainly through woodcut) was one of the earliest forms of illustrations for books and all sorts of prints are used as a way of communicating a particular narrative.

In this project choose a 'story' or scene from a book that you wish to illustrate by the creation of a multi-colour linoprint using the key-block method of registration.

This image can be a depiction of a fairytale, a scene from Shakespeare or even a character from your favourite work of literature. Your piece can tell a story and create a narrative within the image or provide your interpretation of the scene you choose to illustrate.

Think about the style that you use for your print. A colourful bold image may work well with a children's story or the use of darker colours and more stylised marks could be more suitable for a darker or more serious work.

Plan your print using a colour sketch before you start cutting and use several pieces of lino for your blocks. Create the key-block first and then the other colours. You may need to think about including text or titling the print with a quote from your book.

Create a larger edition of 16-20 good final prints.

For the more adventurous, why not try some of the following:

- Create series of illustrations for a whole book
- Design a book cover
- Create some small images to illustrate a poem
- Turn your series of illustrations into an artist's book

Take a look at the following book if you wish to investigate artists' books further:

Creating Artists' Books (Printmaking Handbooks)
by Sarah Bodman
ISBN: 9780713665093

Example Work

'CANDLE' (LINOCUT), SUSAN YEATES, 2006 - 7CM x 7CM. THIS PRINT WAS INSPIRED BY SOME LINES FROM A POEM:

"A CANDLE BURNED ON THE TABLE,
A CANDLE BURNED."

Project 4: A Patchwork Print

About this project

"This project is very popular in 'live' classes and is fantastic as a group exercise or as a way of trying out different techniques on small manageable blocks."

Let's Get Started...

A 'Patchwork Print' is essentially a large relief print created from smaller even-sized blocks that are printed next to each other on a large sheet of paper to create a patchwork.

Choose the size that you want your 'patches' to be – we recommend 7cm or 8cm square. Prepare several sheets of larger printing paper that will fit your image comfortably and draw a grid in pencil where your patches will be placed (see diagram below). A good number of patches to use is either 9 or 16.

grid for printing

Then create a series of small lino prints from blocks that are the size of your patches. You may wish to stick to a theme for them all, a certain colour scheme or make them a complete mixture of styles and images.

Some of your patches may be one colour and some contain many colours. Try using different techniques such as reduction, key-block or 'rainbow rolling' on the different patches to create an interesting contrast.

When your patches are prepared, ink up one patch and print onto your prepared pencil grid by pressing the patch face down onto the paper. Use the pencil lines as a guide for registration ('cheats' registration). If you are using a press, then place this through the press. If you are hand-burnishing, turn the paper over and burnish the back of the paper. Print this patch onto all the pieces of paper and leave to dry. Then repeat with all of the other patches to complete the print. You may wish to have every print identical or change the placement of the patches on each print in the edition.

Example Work

'A Patchwork Print' - created at a workshop in Farnham, Surrey in 2010

Note: This print had 16 patches all 8cm x 8cm in size. The edition of 16 prints was created by a group of students contributing 1 or 2 patches per person. Each print was unique because although they all had the same 'patches' on, they were printed in a different location on the grid on each print.

Useful Resources

Print Studios and Workshops

Artichoke Printmaking, London - www.artichokeprintmaking.com

Badger Press, Bishops Waltham - www.badgerpress.org

Bath Artist Printmakers - www.bathartistprintmakers.com

Birmingham Printmakers - www.birminghamprintmakers.org

Brighton Independent Printmaking - www.brightonprintmaking.co.uk

Cork Printmakers - www.corkprintmakers.ie

Curwen Print Study Centre - www.curwenprintstudy.co.uk

Double Elephant Print Workshop, Exeter - www.doubleelephant.org.uk

Edinburgh Printmakers - www.edinburgh-printmakers.co.uk

Gloucestershire Printmaking Co-Operative - www.gpchq.org

Green Door Printmaking, Derby - www.greendoor-printmaking.co.uk/

handPRINT Studio Printmaking Workshop, Penzance - www.handprintstudio.co.uk

Horsley Printmakers - www.horsleyprintmakers.co.uk

Hot Bed Press, Salford - www.hotbedpress.org

Leicester Print Workshop - www.leicesterprintworkshop.com

London Print Studio - www.londonprintstudio.org.uk

North Notts Non-toxic Printmaking Workshop - www.nontoxicprintmaking.co.uk

Northern Print - www.northernprint.org.uk

Ochre Print Studio, Guildford - www.ochreprintstudio.co.uk

Oxford Printmakers - www.oxfordprintmakers.co.uk

Poole Printmakers, Poole, Dorset - www.poole-printmakers.org.uk

Peacock Visual Arts, Aberdeen - www.peacockvisualarts.co.uk

Red Hot Press, Southampton - www.redhotpress.org.uk

St Barnabas Press, Cambridge - www.stbarnabaspress.co.uk

Spike Print Studio, Bristol - www.spikeprintstudio.org

Societies

East London Printmakers - www.eastlondonprintmakers.co.uk

Greenwich Printmakers - www.greenwich-printmakers.org.uk

For Arts Sake - www.forartssake.com

The Printmakers Council - www.printmaker.co.uk

The Royal Society of Painter-Printmakers - www.banksidegallery.com

Society of Wood Engravers - www.woodengravers.co.uk

Southbank Printmakers - www.southbank-printmakers.com

Periodicals / Magazines

Printmaking Today - www.printmakingtoday.co.uk

Print Quarterly - www.printquarterly.com

Journal of the Print World - www.journalofthe printworld.com

Picture Framers

Otters Pool Studio - www.otterspoolstudio.co.uk

Useful Resources

Materials

Intaglio Printmaker - www.intaglioprintmaker.com

T.N. Lawrence & Son Ltd - www.lawrence.co.uk

Great Art - www.greatart.co.uk

JPP John Purcell Paper - www.johnpurcell.net

Hawthorne Printmaker Supplies - www.hawthornprintmaker.co.uk

Books

The Encyclopedia of Printmaking Techniques
by Judy Martin
ISBN: 0855329874

The Instant Printmaker
by Melvyn Petterson and Colin Gale
ISBN: 1-84340-009-X

Printmakers' Secrets
by Anthony Dyson
ISBN: 0713689110

Practical Printmaking
Edited by Louise Woods
ISBN 0-7134-8830-1

Printmaking for Beginners (Printmaking Handbook S.)
by Jane Stobart
ISBN: 0713650370

Relief Printing (Printmaking Handbook S.)
by Anne Westley
ISBN: 9780713672558

Printmaking: A Contemporary Perspective
by Paul Coldwell
ISBN: 9781906155438

Simple Printmaking
by Gwen Diehn
ISBN: 1579903126

Woodcut Printmaking and Related Techniques
by Walter Chamberlain
ISBN: 0500670137

Handmade Prints
by Anne Desmet and Jim Anderson
ISBN: 0-7136-7708-2

Linoleum Block Printing
by Francis J Kafka
ISBN: 0486203085

The Woodcut Artists Handbook
by George A Walker
ISBN: 1-55407-045-7

Wood Engraving and Linocutting
by Anne Hayward
ISBN: 1861269986

Artists' Websites

Gail Brodholt - www.gailbrodholt.com

Paul Catherall - www.paulcatherall.com

Linda M Farquharson - www.linocut.co.uk

Celia Hart - www.celiahart.co.uk

Mike and Andy Johnson - www.blackandwhitelinocutbrothers.co.uk

Angie Lewin - www.angielewin.co.uk

Nick Morley - www.nickmorley.co.uk

Elizabeth Rashley - www.elizabethrashley.com

Colin Moore - www.colinmoore.uk.com

Tobias Till - www.tobias-till.co.uk

Liz Toole - www.liztoole.co.uk

Susan Yeates - www.magenta-sky.com